DICK, THE BABYSITTING BEAR

and Other Great Wild Animal Stories

Other books in the series
The Good Lord Made Them All
by Joe L. Wheeler

Owney, the Post Office Dog
and Other Great Dog Stories

Smoky, the Ugliest Cat in the World
and Other Great Cat Stories

Wildfire, the Red Stallion
and Other Great Horse Stories

DICK, THE BABYSITTING BEAR

and Other Great Wild Animal Stories

Compiled and edited by
Joe L. Wheeler

Pacific Press® Publishing Association
Nampa, Idaho
Oshawa, Ontario, Canada
www.pacificpress.com

Cover art by Lars Justinen
Designed by Justinen Creative Group
Interior illustrations from the library of Joe L. Wheeler

Additional copies of this book are available by calling toll free 1-800-765-6955 or by visiting http://www.adventistbookcenter.com

Library of Congress Cataloging-in-Publication Data

Dick, the babysitting bear : and other great wild animal stories / compiled and edited by Joe L. Wheeler.
p. cm.
ISBN-13: 978-0-8163-2221-3 (paper back)
ISBN-10: 0-8163-2221-X
1. Animals—Anecdotes. I. Wheeler, Joe L., 1936-
QL791.D526 2007
590—dc22
2007034159

www.joewheelerbooks.com

07 08 09 10 11 • 5 4 3 2 1

Contents

DEDICATION

This is a first for me. Never before have I dedicated a book to someone who has had a huge impact on my books in two separate publishing houses. Not only that, but someone who helped me give birth to two separate series of books.

She was one of the two individuals most responsible for the success of the Christmas in My Heart series (now in its sixteenth annual collection) with Review and Herald® Publishing Association. When she moved to Pacific Press® Publishing Association, her visionary eye saw the same potential in the series The Good Lord Made Them All (now in its fourth annual collection).

So it gives me great pleasure to dedicate this book to a woman who not only changed my life but who has also had a significant impact upon the lives of all those readers who so love the stories in these twenty collections (so far):
SUSAN HARVEY

INTRODUCTION
Life's Defining Moments

Joseph Leininger Wheeler

It was a stunningly beautiful first day of April 2004 at the Harris Neck Wildlife Refuge on the Georgia coast. All around us was serenity: white herons by the score, ducks of many kinds, dozing alligators and turtles, seabirds flying overhead.

As we leisurely strolled along an embankment, the moment came—completely unannounced. Had we been looking any other direction in the lagoon, we'd have missed it, for the entire scene took

only a split second. At a speed one wouldn't have believed possible in such a sluggish-looking beast, a great alligator leaped out of the water at one of the largest birds on the Georgia coast, a condor-sized buzzard placidly sunning himself. As he was seized in those implacable jaws, the wings shot out in a futile attempt to fly away, and a millisecond later there was an empty space where the bird had been and barely a ripple to mark the spot where the alligator had attacked.

A professional nature photographer standing next to us completely missed the shot of a lifetime, so quickly did it happen. His wife turned to us and said, "Such attacks usually take place at night so they're almost never seen by the human eye—in all our years of photographing wildlife on this coast, that was an absolute first for us!"

The six of us who'd seen it just stood there in a state of shock— one moment vibrant life, the next, a bone-crunching death deep in the lagoon. Not often in this fast-paced life in which we live is the veil between life and death so transparently thin. The only personal comparable I can think of occurred early one evening on a narrow Colorado river road seven years ago when an out-of-control driver lost his trajectory on a curve and smashed into my wife and me, totaling both vehicles. In the split second between seeing those headlights veering across the center line and the crash, we assumed we were breathing the last breath God would grant us in this life . . . but we lived through it.

The result of both experiences has been a heightened appreciation of how incredibly fragile is this thread we glibly label "life"—and how little it takes to snap it!

Such defining moments we call "epiphanies." One moment the train of life is barreling down a set of tracks in one direction; the next, it's racing down a new set of tracks in an entirely different direction. Rarely do we realize we're experiencing a life-changing epiphany; only in retrospect do we see how different our lives would have been had that day not taken place.

For my wife and me, the two experiences, four years apart, have resulted in a heightened awareness of life, of the need to savor to the utmost every day, hour, minute, and second God grants us, recognizing that each comes but once. Not all the gold in Fort Knox can buy back a millisecond of life.

One of the tragedies of our age has to do with the way we waste the only bullion that matters—Time. Waste it staring glassy-eyed at the television set, text-messaging inanities on our cell phones, exchanging trivialities on the Web—oh, the list is endless. Majoring in minors, that's what so many of us do with our lives, and we discover, belatedly, that though we took the normal number of breaths, we *never really lived!*

The stories featured in this book, as well as the stories in the other collections in *The Good Lord Made Them All* series, represent moments of heightened awareness, defining moments, if you will; attempts to stop the clock of time long enough to internalize value for what has just been experienced (be it actual or vicarious, matters little, as the mind has a difficult time differentiating between the two).

My prayer is that these stories will help us become more aware of the interconnectedness of all God's creatures.

About this collection

Every attempt has been made to gather one of the most powerful collections of wild animal stories ever gathered between two covers. Even though this book features headliners such as Zane Grey, Penny Porter, and Ernest Thompson Seton, the power of the story alone has been the deciding factor in determining which stories made the cut.

A wide variety of animal protagonists can be found in these pages—bears, rabbits, raccoons, moose, elephants, buffaloes, blacksnakes, razorbacks, coyotes—even barn swallows and a peacock.

If there is a theme, it is the interconnectedness of all created beings.

CODA

I look forward to hearing from you! I always welcome the stories, responses, and suggestions that are sent to us from our readers. I am putting together collections centered on other genres as well. You may reach me by writing to:

Joe L. Wheeler, PhD
P.O. Box 1246
Conifer, CO 80433

* * * * *

"Life's Defining Moments," by Joseph Leininger Wheeler. Copyright © 2007. Printed by permission of the author.

Dick, the Babysitting Bear

Floyd Bralliar

This pre–Civil War narrative is one of the earliest of true stories about bear cubs. Dick was born in the Ozark Mountains more than a hundred and fifty years ago. Generations of readers have laughed at his antics ever since the story was anthologized in Elo the Eagle and Other Stories *in 1947.*

* * * * *

Years ago, on the side of one of the Ozark Mountains, about twenty miles south of the present city of Springfield, Missouri, stood a schoolhouse the like of which very few of the present generation have ever seen.

At that time only a few families had moved into the country, and everything was crude and undeveloped; but with a desire to educate their children that has made America the foremost nation in the world in matters educational, these pioneers determined to have a school. Circumstances could scarcely have been more unfavorable or fewer facilities at hand. Nevertheless, undaunted by the difficulties in the way, they chose a place as nearly central as could be found and prepared to build their first schoolhouse.

Logs were cut and dragged to the site, the ends being notched so they would stay in position, were laid up to form the walls. Chips, twigs, and even small limbs were stuffed into the cracks between the logs. On one side of the room, window space was sawed out, and as there was no glass to put in it, ventilation was assured.

Clapboards fastened to cross logs with wooden pins—for nails were high priced, and difficult to get at any price—formed the roof. These clapboards were boards split from the side of a log with an ax, and quite unsmoothed. You can readily see that they would not fit closely enough together to make a water-tight roof; but as other boards had to be sawed with a handsaw, they were too expensive to use for this purpose. The door was likewise made of clapboards, and hung upon hinges made from strips of raw deerskin. When the mountain rats dined on these hinges, as they occasionally did, new ones were put on.

Desks and tables, there were none. A split log, flat side up, was fastened to the wall on one side of the room, and here the children could stand to write. The seats were crude affairs, made by splitting logs as nearly in the middle as possible, and putting in wooden pins on the rounded side for legs—not much to look at when compared with the cleverly adjusted, rubber-hinged, and finely polished wonders that adorn the modern schoolroom. Nevertheless, the children who gathered there to study and recite had eyes as bright, cheeks as rosy, brains as active and alert, plans and dreams as ambitious, and hearts as happy and hopeful and loving as any schoolchildren on the round earth today. They made the most of every advantage and the best of every disadvantage, and their later life proved that they had learned well the early lessons taught by hardship and privation.

The schoolroom was heated with a fireplace, so arranged that the children could cluster around it on cold days and be out of the direct draft of the window. The chimney was a crude affair, built of sticks laid up corncob-pen fashion. No school was held in the winter on account of the cold, and as it was usually warm enough at other seasons to get along without more than an occasional fire, the heating arrangements answered every purpose.

Just in front of the door ran the road, where a place in the dust was kept smooth for a blackboard. The writing was done with sharply pointed sticks. Rains sometimes made it inconvenient to erase the work for a day or two, but as the earth hardened, the boys would loosen it, the sun would dry it, and then it was easily reduced to dust again. The abundant flat rocks were substituted for slates, and what boy or girl would use a slate pencil when there was an abundance of red and yellow keel to be had for the picking up?

The children had no schoolbooks, at least not in our understanding of the term, but Grandfather Hornbeak had brought a number of newspapers with him from Nashville, Tennessee, and these were placed at the disposal of the teacher. Being a woman of resource, she cut them in pieces and pasted letters, words, and even sentences on thin boards, thus providing every pupil with a "book" adapted to his years and attainments. Ink was prepared from the nutgalls that grew on the white oaks, and a turkey quill made an excellent pen.

Back of the schoolhouse the mountains rose bold and rocky, covered in places with heavy timber. About a hundred rods (1,650 feet) from the back of the building, in the side of the mountain, was a small cave, in which two black bears had their den. Their cubs used to come out and tumble and play by the hour in plain sight of the schoolhouse window; and the old bears even ventured to come down and eat the scraps of corn bread that were sometimes scattered about the door.

One day, when one of the old bears came down to the schoolhouse for something to eat, leaving her cubs sitting by the den to wait for their share, one of the cubs decided to follow her. The old bear did not see him until he was by her side, just under the window. With a growl, she caught him under one paw, and sitting down on her haunches, turned him over her knee and proceeded to give the surprised fellow such a spanking as no boy ever received. He howled and screamed for mercy, and when he was finally released, scampered back to the den with all possible haste, whimpering and crying as he went, a wiser and more obedient cub. Needless to say, he remembered his lesson and never again followed his mother to the schoolhouse. Bears are proverbially cross when they have young, so the children were allowed to play only in the road in front of the door. Parents always accompanied the children to school in the morning and came for them at the close of the session. There were so many wild beasts in the woods that it was not safe for them to go back and forth by themselves.

Things ran on in this way for some time, the old bears growing more ferocious each year, until one spring it was decided that they must be caught. Accordingly, traps were set, and the old bears and two cubs were captured. The reader may wonder why this was not done sooner. The reason is simple enough. The people depended on bears and deer for meat, and it was not only a waste to kill an old bear, whose flesh was too strong to eat, but it lessened the number of cubs that would be raised in the vicinity every year. Game was not killed merely for sport in those days.

One of these captured bear cubs, Dick, was taken for a pet by my mother's father. It is Dick's life history I mean to tell, just as my mother, who was then a little girl, has often told it to me.

At first, Dick was sullen and refused to eat, and had to be kept chained to a tree in the yard. Here he amused himself by lying perfectly quiet beside his food until a cat or a chicken stole up to eat it; then he would suddenly slap the intruder over. Young bears, like sullen children, soon come to their appetite if left alone, and it was not long until Dick ate quite heartily enough to satisfy his owner, and grew fat and good-natured. He was soon very tame, and was allowed to run about at his own sweet will. Now began his fun and mischief-making. He had an enormous appetite, so naturally his first mischief was in stealing forbidden food. Cream and butter were his favorite dainties, but for some reason he could never understand, he was usually given only milk, which he drank simply for courtesy's sake and because he could do no better. But Dick, though only a young bear, was no fool.

Around the point of the hill, at some distance from the house, was a deep spring, and there had been built a log milk house, which was thought to be proof against all wild beasts. But Dick was no common bear. He had not been born and brought up in plain sight of the only schoolhouse in the country for nothing! In those days, doors were made to close and catch with a strong latch on the inside. A string was fastened to this latch and passed out through a hole in the door, so that by pulling the string one could lift the latch. All the doors in the house were locked simply by drawing the latchstrings inside. Dick delighted to come into the house and sleep on the hearth, but as he was often much in the way, this privilege was usually denied him. He was a keen observer, however, and soon learned to pull the latchstring himself and open the door at will.

One day when Dick was passing the milk house, he smelled the appetizing odor of fresh butter and milk and immediately set out to investigate. He walked around the house, inspecting every part. He climbed on the roof and tried to move the boards; he got down and examined the stream running from under the house to see if that offered a solution to the question he wished to solve. Finally, he found the door, and the rest was easy. Promptly raising himself on his haunches, he pulled the latchstring and opened the door. What a time he had then! No milk for him! He licked the thick cream from crock after crock, and then, to show how little he thought of skim milk, dumped it into the water. This was fun, but very mild amusement compared to what followed when he found the butter. When he was discovered, the butter jar was wiped clean, and he was so full he could scarcely waddle. Of course he was whipped, but though he howled so loudly that those who listened could not but believe his repentance was heartfelt, he repeated the experiment a night or two later. This time, however, he decided not to upset the milk, since stupid humans seemed to think it of so much value!

Thereafter, Dick's raids on the milk house continued until the latch was placed beyond his reach. Then he would watch till the door was left ajar, dash in, drink cream as fast as he could until discovered, and when sure that he was seen, grab a crock of butter and run. But he had no use for salted butter; it seemed queer to him that anyone would spoil so delicious a luxury as fresh butter by mixing salt with it. However, he was seldom annoyed in this way, for all the salt used in those days was brought 150 miles by wagon over an unsettled mountain country.

Just after dark one evening, one of the girls went to the milk house to bring up milk and butter for supper. Dick was loitering about, as usual, watching for an opportunity to enter, when a panther came near. The coveted dainty instantly lost its charms for Dick in this unwelcome presence, and with more haste than dignity, he waddled off in the direction of the house, climbing to the top of the tallest tree in the yard. The girl, my aunt, was naturally frightened, but with the nerve and foresight of every girl born on the frontier, she went quietly on and finished getting her cream and butter even when the great beast jumped on the roof of the milk house. Coming out, she closed the door firmly and started up the hill.

It was an unpleasant moment. The great cat jumped over her head, lighting at her side, but she walked on as if nothing had happened. He followed, frisking about her, jumping over her, back and forth, even striking her in the face with his tail; but he did not harm her. As they neared the house, the great watchdog (a half-breed gray wolf) rushed out, and the panther fled up the nearest tree, which happened to be the one where the pet bear was hiding. Without a moment's hesitation, Dick tumbled out and down and scampered away to take refuge in another tree on the opposite side of the yard.

The thoroughly frightened girl rushed into the house and told her story, but the panther was not troubled till morning, the dog keeping guard about his tree. Panthers have an instinctive and unreasoning fear of dogs. The least puppy will tree a panther, and there he will stay till the dog goes away. In the morning the unwelcome visitor was shot, but was only wounded, and so made his escape to the woods. Dick acted as if mortally afraid of him, and never again ventured far into the forest where such animals run wild. Indeed, so great was his fear that when he heard a panther scream far up the side of the mountain, he would come close to the house door and beg to be let in.

Another of Dick's failings was his love for fruits and vegetables. He would risk a whipping any day for the sake of a fragrant muskmelon or a juicy watermelon. A sound thrashing he counted a small price for the privilege of gorging himself on roasting ears. Indeed, it was difficult for the farmers to raise corn in those days, for the wild bears were almost sure to despoil the fields completely at roasting-ear time.

Grandfather Hornbeak kept bees, and it was a never-failing pleasure to Dick to tease and annoy them. He would sit at the side of the hives by the hour and strike and fight and kill the busy workers, all the time whining as if very much abused. However, if they ceased flying about him in interesting numbers, he would hit the hive smartly to stir them up again. Flowers were so plentiful and honey was so easy to get that the bees often built combs on the bottom and sides of their hives, but after Dick came to the farmyard to live, all this stopped. He kept the comb broken off close and the drops of sweetness licked clean, for there is nothing that a bear likes quite so well as honey. Wild bees sometimes built combs in the corners of the rail fences in the peach orchard, and it was Dick's delight to find and rob such a nest.

Honey was so plentiful that it was served with every meal, and the ever-watchful bear soon found this out. At mealtime he was always loitering about the door, and if the slightest opportunity offered itself as the table was being laid, he would grab the honey dish and waddle off with it. The womenfolk soon found that to follow him meant only that the dish would be broken—but if he were left alone he would lick it clean, bring it back, and set it carefully on the porch. It soon became evident that no amount of whipping would cure him of the honey habit; consequently, if he once got hold of the honey, he was left alone till he finished it—and usually afterward. The only thing was to keep the honey dish where he could not get it, and then see that he did not come into the house.

Near the farm ran Findley Creek, which Dick visited every day for a bath and a frolic. One of his keenest delights was to find a shallow place where he could make a regular loblolly of mud. Here he would play and roll and sleep for hours like a hog, but unlike a hog he always went into the water afterward and washed himself clean.

Hogs were few and far between in those days; the only way they could be raised at all was to keep them in a bear-proof pen. This was made by building a high pen of logs, with a roof of the same, slanting toward the middle. Thus an animal could get on top of the pen and drop in, but he could not get out again. This was exactly what the farmers wanted, as a bear is very careful not to kill anything where he cannot get away afterward.

One night, the spirit of mischief—or the spirit of pilfering—entered into Dick, and he decided that one of the week-old pigs in the pen was just what he wanted. The pen was near; it was no trick at all to climb in. But that was not the end of the story. The old sow was of that peculiar variety known as "razorback," an animal almost equal to the lion in a fight. But Dick cared nothing at all for that. He was not looking for a fight—just for a baby pig. So in he climbed and caught one.

In the morning, it was noticed that something unusual was going on in the pig pen. When Grandfather arrived at the center of the storm, Dick was sitting up in one corner with a little pig in his arms. He would sway back and forth, rocking it gently till it became quiet; then he would box its head or nibble its ear to make it squeal. Naturally enough, this proceeding worked the old sow up to a frenzy, and she would attack him, only to be slapped over as soon and as often as she came within range of his powerful paw. Every little while, appearing to see the hopelessness of the fight, she would retreat to her corner, and Dick would rock and lick the little pig as tenderly as if it were the dearest thing in the world. Then when all was quiet, he would slyly bite its ear again. When he was found and realized that the pig was to be taken from him, he was ready for a real fight. For a while it looked as if he would have to be killed, but a whipping was all that was needed to straighten the matter out. Afterward he was taken to the house, where he sulked for a day or two, but he never climbed into the pig pen again.

There was another thing that gave Dick great delight for a time, but soon got him into trouble. The dogs in the neighborhood were trained to tree bears. This suited Dick very well since he knew just how to handle dogs. He would get several after him, running till they came close. Then he would turn around, plant his back against a tree, and slap them over as fast as they came near enough. This was great sport for Dick. He learned that he could manage any number of dogs if he could get his back against a tree.

But alas for pride! A bench-legged bulldog, with a consuming ambition to hunt bears, was brought into the neighborhood. Then Dick's troubles began in earnest. The other dogs were tall and easy to get at; but while Dick was boxing them, this little stranger would come up, seize him by the haunch, and there was no way to get rid of him but to climb a tree—not an easy thing to do with half a dozen dogs ready to grab him as soon as his back was turned. Nor could Dick remedy the matter, for the bulldog was so low that Dick could not easily reach him to box him over. Things became so uncomfortable for the bear that he ceased to encourage these hunting parties; indeed, he thereafter avoided all places that contained dogs.

With cats, it was different. Dick caught a cat every time he had a chance, stroking it, smoothing its fur, and making as much fuss over it as any girl—as long as it behaved. But if it dared to bite or scratch, he would spank it unmercifully. No matter how much it snarled and spit and scratched, he would not let it go until it quieted down and allowed him to play with it. Often that meant that it was dead. The cats soon came to know and avoid him—all but the household pet, who learned that Dick did not mean her any harm and enjoyed having him stroke and play with her.

Toward fall, a strange feeling came over Dick. One day he stood by one of his favorite trees, and putting his arms around it as if preparing to climb, began scratching and biting and tearing the bark as high as he could reach until his mouth frothed, and he became exhausted. Thus, perhaps unknowingly, he posted a sign to everyone of his own tribe who might pass that way that there was a male bear in the neighborhood—and informed them just how tall he was and hence how powerful in battle he was likely to be. For a time, he repeated this often. But as no other bears came near the house, he gradually ceased these demonstrations and did not renew them till the same season next year. Later, when he was installed as head of Grandfather Farrer's bear ranch, he would fly into a tremendous rage if he happened to find a similar mark made by one of his own cubs.

There was one trick of his youth that Dick never forgot, and that was how to catch chickens, but in his old age he ate them as well. Taking something the chickens liked to eat, he would go where they were likely to gather, taking good care that the chosen spot was out of sight of the house. Then Dick would place his bait, sit down near it, and pretend to go to sleep—all but his eyes, which the chickens were too stupid to watch. I am told that a wild chicken is a very wise and wary bird, but long generations of domestication have certainly taken all this out of our barnyard fowls, till they are as stupid as any creature I know. Dick would sit still as a stump till a hen came within range of his paw. One slap was enough to ensure his dinner, for he never missed. When he had eaten all he wished, he would go off innocently about his business.

Just so, a wild bear on the mountain ranges learns to kill cattle. Going out in plain sight of a herd and in such a way that the wind blows from him toward them, he will stand straight up on his haunches. Of course the cattle run, but when they notice that he does not follow them, they circle about and come back nearer and nearer to see what it all means. Closer and yet closer they come, smelling and sniffing. Presently one will leave the herd and steal up within range. Then the hitherto statue hurls his thunderbolt of a paw at its jaw, and the cowboys tell me that they have never known one to escape after it has once been slapped. Of course, the rest of the cattle run when this happens and leave the bear to finish his victim in peace.

Whenever Dick got into too much mischief, he was whipped—sometimes quite severely. It did not take him long to learn which of his offenses brought punishment, and when he was discovered in some forbidden prank, he would run and climb to the top of a tall blackjack tree that stood in the yard. Here he was reasonably secure, as no amount of shaking would dislodge him. There was only one way to get him down—to pelt him with rocks. When this was begun, he would whine and try to hide, but finally he would slide down to take his punishment with what grace he could muster.

There was one strictly forbidden thing that Dick particularly enjoyed—taking care of the baby. He would rock the cradle, lick the baby, and manifest his pleasure in it in every way he knew, but he was altogether too fond of putting into practice the old saying about not sparing the rod. Sometimes he would decide to spank the baby, and spank it he would, despite all protests.

Grandfather Farrer had a bear ranch. That was not what he called it, but that is what it would be called now. It consisted of a large enclosure or pen, where he raised bears to kill for meat. In this way he not only had all the bear meat he wished for his own use, but sold both bear bacon and bear lard. Dick was installed as the head of this family living in the enclosure. The mother bears and their cubs were allowed to run loose in the pen, but as Dick grew older, he became so vicious that he was kept chained. He could go in and out of his own log house at will, but no farther.

These bears were a great attraction to the children, even in this wild country, and whenever the neighbors came to the house to visit, the children always flocked out to watch the bears at play. But at last Dick grew so ill-natured that they were forbidden to enter the pen.

One well-remembered day Grandmother Hornbeak made a visit to the Farrer house. While the women were busy in one room, the baby slept in a cradle in another. It was a warm day, and the door stood open. Dick had been restless all day. Finally he slipped his chain, and unseen by anyone, went straight to the house, entered the room where the baby was sleeping, and carried it off. Had he been a wise bear, according to bear standards of wisdom, he would have gone to the woods; instead, he took the baby to his house in the bear pen, and going to the corner farthest from the door, sat up on his haunches to rock it. Just how long he held it, no one knows, but the baby finally awakened and began to cry. Grandmother Hornbeak heard the child crying; that was the first she had missed the baby.

You can imagine how frightened they all were when it was known that Dick—who had grown so cross that it was hardly safe for a man to come too close—had stolen the baby. The men were summoned from the field, and as soon as Dick saw them, he began to growl. The poor baby was frightened, too, as well it might be, and began crying afresh at the top of its voice. Then the bear swayed back and forth, rocking it, licking its face, and apparently trying to soothe it. He seemed to understand that the men would try harder to get the child if it cried.

For several hours they coaxed and threatened and did everything they could think of—all to no avail. Finally, the baby fell asleep. Dick held it as gently as he could and acted as if afraid of awakening it. Grandfather Farrer proposed shooting Dick, but the others would not hear of that. They thought it would mean almost certain death to the little one. Finally, they went to the deer park (Grandfather Farrer raised deer as well as bears) and brought a little fawn, which they tied as far from the bear's house as they could and yet have it in plain sight at the same time.

At first, Dick paid no attention to the fawn, but finally he laid the sleeping babe carefully down and ran to get the little deer. Then the men quickly jumped through the window into Dick's house and picked up the child. Dick was greatly enraged when he saw the trick that had been played on him, and even after he had partly quieted down, he had to be whipped.

A few nights later, Dick got loose again; and though it almost staggers belief, yet it is actually true that he went a mile and a half, pulled the latchstring, entered the Hornbeak cabin, stole the same babe out of its sleeping mother's arms, and carried it to his den. The parents were frantic when they found that the child was gone. And you may well imagine that when they learned in whose care it was, they did not feel greatly relieved. Dick was furious this time when discovered. But the child was finally rescued once more, and after that Dick did not get loose again.

Finally, Dick did a terrible thing, and had to be put down. But he had lived a long time, and had been in many ways, a remarkable member of the bear family. It was his misfortune that he was judged by human standards, standards his bear mind found impossible to understand.

* * * * *

"Dick, the Babysitting Bear," by Floyd Bralliar. Included in Bralliar's book, Elo the Eagle and Other Stories *(Washington, D.C.: Review and Herald® Publishing Association, 1947). Reprinted by permission of Joe Wheeler (P.O. Box 1246, Conifer, CO 80433) and Review and Herald® Publishing Association, Hagerstown, MD 20740. Floyd Bralliar wrote around the turn of the twentieth century.*

Bounce and Miss Gibbs

Eleanor Stimson Brooks

*Daddy was going to shoot the rabbits that were wrecking his garden,
but Peter begged him to save the life of two of the perpetrators.
Who could have known how the rabbits would repay that debt?*

* * * * *

"*Sh-h-h!*" said Peter, and then, in a loud, agitated whisper, "*Sh-h-h!*
Oh look, Mother, do look, quick, but don't move! There they are—
those are my pet rabbits!"

Peter and his mother were sitting together, eating breakfast, in
the big, cheerful kitchen of their new midwestern home; and the
spring sunshine, slipping through the open window, fell full on
Peter, his sandy-colored head bobbing with excitement, his little
eight-year-old figure nearly swallowed up by enveloping blue
overalls, and on his mother, still flushed from her work over the
stove. She turned cautiously and looked out where Peter's stubby
finger pointed.

The little lawn about the home ended here at the back, in a small
kitchen garden where young lettuce, turnips, cabbages, and other
vegetables showed temptingly through a screen of chicken wire. To

one side lay acres and acres of plowed land, already green with the young wheat, and back of them stretched miles of open prairie, now lovely with new grass and the first spring wildflowers. Close by the wire, their eager, sensitive little noses hunting over it for an opening, were two small brown rabbits.

"How," whispered Mrs. Rawdon, ". . . how do you know those are your pets, dear? They look just like all the other wild rabbits to me."

"Why, can't you see?" protested Peter, indignantly. "Miss Gibbs is much bigger than any of the other rabbits" (Miss Gibbs was so named as a compliment to the new primary teacher), "and Bounce has lost the tip of his left ear. I think a dog must have nearly caught him once."

"Well, I must say," sighed Mrs. Rawdon, "I wish they and the other rabbits would let my garden alone. I take such pains with it, and then just as something is ready for the table, they manage somehow to get under that wire, and the next day there is nothing left but stalks."

Peter's little face took on a look of anxiety mingled with mortification, so his mother added hastily, "Will they take things out of your hands yet, honey pot? They seem very wild for pets."

"They *almost* will," declared Peter, proudly. "You know, Mother, you said I could have a few of the biggest lettuce leaves and some of the turnips and carrots. They are *very* fond of turnips. I've been trying for weeks now, and yesterday Miss Gibbs really nibbled off the end of a turnip while I was holding it and while I kept quite still; but when I tried to pet her, she ran away. Oh! Oh! Look at them now!"

The little rabbits were standing on their hind legs, vainly trying to reach over the wire. Then, either giving up in despair or seized by some wild impulse, they suddenly dropped down and began frolicking like kittens. Such leaps and scurries! Such twinkling little feet, bobbing ears, sudden alarms! Peter was just thinking it the prettiest play in the world when his oatmeal spoon, which had stopped halfway to his mouth ten minutes before, slipped from his fingers and fell with a deafening clatter upon the table. There was a flash of white tails, and in a moment both of the bunnies were out of sight in the grass.

"There!" cried the little boy, disgustedly. "I frightened them away."

"Frightened off some wild rabbits?" asked Peter's father, appearing at that moment in the doorway. "Good for you! And that reminds me, Mother," he went on, "we are through with the heaviest of the spring work at last; tonight I'll sit up with my gun and shoot every rabbit that dares show his whiskers about your garden."

If Peter's father had expected this news to be received with pleasure, he had made a mistake. Mrs. Rawdon threw an anxious glance at Peter, and as for Peter himself his lips quivered, his eyes filled, and he broke into a wail of protest. "Oh, Daddy," he begged, "please don't shoot the rabbits tonight! In the dark you can't tell what you hit, and two of them are my very particular friends. I am sure I could catch them and make pets of them if I had a trap. Please wait!"

Peter's father looked surprised, but sympathetic. "All right, son," he reassured him. "We'll put off shooting until tomorrow, and I'll help you make the trap."

It was lucky for Peter, but even more so for Bounce and Miss Gibbs that the two little rabbits had developed a taste for turnips. The trap was baited with the tenderest ones the garden afforded, and before the afternoon was over, both little animals—fat, frightened, and indignant—were caught and safely transferred to a new little rabbit hutch which Peter himself had helped to make.

For the next ten days, Bounce and Miss Gibbs were dreadfully wild. When anyone appeared, they would rush to the farthest, darkest corner of their hutch and hide until the intruder was gone again. As for petting or even holding them, it was out of the question. Peter learned, to his hurt astonishment, that rabbits have claws and a tremendous kick in their hind legs. But before long his devotion and the quantities of good things he gave them to eat began to take effect, and by the time the wheat was grown and was beginning to turn a beautiful golden yellow, the two bunnies would follow him about like dogs. Whenever he appeared, they would come hopping happily along the side of their hutch to meet him, Miss Gibbs larger than ever, Bounce flopping his scarred ear.

Some people think a rabbit has no voice. Peter found his rabbits had; for whenever they were hungry, they would scurry to his feet and make the funniest little sound, half a squeak, half a whimper, which said quite plainly, "Dinner, please, at once!" He patiently taught them several tricks, and they learned so quickly that everyone considered them to be very clever rabbits. Indeed, Miss Patience, who came to manage the cooking for the harvest hands, was almost afraid of them. One day she saw Miss Gibbs performing her most useful trick, that of thumping on a tin pan for Peter to bring her dinner, since he was too far away to be "squeaked for," and ever after Miss Patience insisted that " 'Twasn't natural for critters to be that knowing." Most of the time the rabbits were kept shut up in their hutch, as they had never outgrown their fondness for the kitchen garden.

The rabbits were an old story by the time the long, hot summer dragged itself to an end. For weeks there had been no rain, and the prairie stretched away a dreary, unbroken expanse of sunbaked grass. The flowers were all dead, the roads choked with dust. The only bits of green were a few carefully watered lawns and gardens and the banks of the little stream which had run so prettily through the town in the spring. The stream itself had dwindled to a mere trickle in the mud, except for one shallow pool under the willows. Then came a day so hot the very earth seemed to crack.

"You poor little bunnies," sighed Peter, "with such heavy fur coats! I'm going to give you each a shower bath." And he did, with his watering can, to the astonishment and terror of the rabbits. "I don't believe you like water," he reflected, watching the results. "Perhaps I had better cut off your long hair instead."

But fortunately his mother came by as he was about to begin, and persuaded him that cutting the fur of a rabbit was really too dangerous. They wriggled so much, he was likely to snip off an ear or a tail instead!

That night when Peter went to bed on the porch, which he shared with his father, he found it very hard to go to sleep. He lay for a long time looking at the stars and listening to the faint, dry rustle of the prairie grass. It must have been long after midnight when he awoke with a great start. What had happened? He sat up in bed confused and sleepy, and it was a minute or two before he realized that there was a great commotion going on in the rabbit hutch, from the midst of which came the *thumpity, thump, thump* of the rabbits on their tin pan. Why were they calling him? He stumbled out of bed and over to the edge of the porch, where he peered down into the dark garden. He could see nothing, but he had the curious feeling that hundreds of things were rushing past him—birds in the air, little animals in the grass, and surely that big black shape which came crashing out of the currant bushes and dashed across the lawn was a cow!

The breeze, which had rustled the grass so gently when he went to sleep, had grown strong and hot, and as he stared over toward the rabbits, he suddenly noticed a long red line which stretched from edge to edge of the horizon, vivid against the dark sky.

"Daddy!" called Peter. "Daddy, come quick! What is it?"

"What is what?" came the deep, startled voice of Peter's father out of the dark. "Don't shout like that, son. . . ." All at once the voice changed and became cool, energetic, and matter-of-fact. "Get dressed at once, Peter," it said, "while I tell Mother. It's a prairie fire, and we must rouse the town."

Peter never forgot the night that followed. It seemed only a moment before he and his father were in the street, beating at doors and shouting the news up to the windows and porches. In a few minutes more, the streets were full of frightened, half-dressed people who gathered anxiously about the only lamp in the square to discuss hurriedly what should be done. Had Peter but known it, the little town of Jonesville was in a truly desperate situation. Ten miles away lay the railroad, the nearest means of safety, but the wind was momentarily growing stronger, and by its help the fire was advancing so rapidly that many doubted if the distance could be covered in time. Then there might not be a train. Besides, there were not horses enough for all, and even if the people could escape, to run away meant to abandon the work of years, their homes, their farms—for many of them, everything they owned in the world.

"There's only one way!" cried a voice in the crowd. It was "Lucky Jake," an old pioneer who had seen the very beginning of Jonesville. "We must make a ring of fire about the town and start it out to meet the one that's coming. Then we shall have a lot of ground around us where there is nothing left to burn. If it's wide enough, the fire can't jump it; it will have to go around. It's mighty lucky for us that the harvest is about in and most of the fields bare, anyhow."

This was quickly decided upon as the wisest—indeed, the only— plan, and every man, woman, and child in the little settlement came out to help. Starting the fire downwind was easy enough, and it was easy also to prevent its burning back into the town. Half a dozen big boys could see to that. But to make it burn *against* the wind! That was a different matter! There was terrible danger of it getting beyond control at any moment and destroying the town at once. The men started the flames in lines, a little at a time, while right behind them stood the women and children with sticks, pails of water, wet brooms and cloths—beating back the flames when they turned toward the houses. They were ably helped by two young men on horseback, holding a dripping blanket stretched between them, who rode up and down the lines continually.

There was plenty of light for what they had to do. To Peter, it seemed as if the whole world were on fire, and the bright flames, the leaping, fantastic shadows, the hurrying black figures seemed to belong to some fairy tale. But although he was very hot and excited and his arms ached with beating back flames, he was hardly frightened at all. He felt such confidence in Father, Jake, and the other men.

After what seemed hours of desperately hard and dangerous work, a broad belt of burned land lay all about them. Mrs. Rawdon had found Peter, and since there was nothing more they could do, they stood hand in hand watching the wall of flame sweep toward them. The wind had now grown very fierce and strong, the smoke denser and denser. Peter's eyes smarted dreadfully, and his throat ached with constant coughing and choking. The fire was almost upon them when Mr. Rawdon appeared and ordered all the women and children into the bed of the creek. "Go down to the old swimming hole," he urged them. "If it gets too hot, get right into the stream—and remember that the air is best close to the ground."

"You come too!" begged Peter. But his father explained that he could not. Big sparks were beginning to fly across the town, and the men wanted to be ready if anything caught fire.

Crouched down in the dark, in the wet mud of the creek, holding tight to his mother's hand, Peter heard the fire come roaring upon them. The air grew hotter and hotter, full of flying sparks and cinders, the smoke denser and denser.

All about them they could hear the crackling and spitting of the grass. Suddenly Peter gave a cry. "Oh, Mother! The rabbits! I forgot them when we started fighting the fire, and it was they that woke me. Please let me go and get them! Please! Please!" And he wept bitterly when his mother, trying to comfort him, explained that the rabbits would surely be all right, but that she couldn't, couldn't let him go to get them.

"How do you suppose they noticed the fire?" Peter asked a few moments later, between sobs. "Do you think they saw it?"

"No . . . no . . . ," hesitated Mrs. Rawdon, "you said you heard the little wild animals rushing across the garden. That must have awakened and frightened the rabbits. Perhaps they smelled the fire also."

The minutes seemed very long there in the heat and the smoke, but it was really barely half an hour before the heat waned, the smoke grew less dense, and they could hear the men shouting that the fire had gone by. Overhead the first faint dawn was breaking, and as they came scrambling up from the bed of the creek, Peter could not help laughing at the queer appearance of his friends. In the gray light they looked more like hobgoblins than people, covered as they were with mud and water grasses, their faces streaked with cinders and still pale with anxiety.

Away off downwind, the fire was disappearing in the direction of the river which would, at last, put an end to its career of destruction.

As soon as Peter and his mother had found his father and made sure he was safe, Peter slipped off by himself and ran as fast as his short legs would take him to the rabbit hutch. How strange the garden looked in the gray dawn, trampled and disordered by the confusion of the past night! But there in one corner was the rabbit hutch, and huddled together inside, frightened but safe, were Miss Gibbs and Bounce, just as his mother had said they would be. With cries of delight and relief Peter flung himself down to pet and caress them. Then he hurried indoors for a market basket, and coming back, he placed the rabbits carefully inside it.
Suddenly it occurred to him that the dim, deserted garden was a very lonely spot for a little boy of eight, and he hurried back to the square.

Although it was growing lighter every moment, the lamp still flickered feebly, and once more the whole town seemed to be gathered around it. Over their tired, thankful faces Peter could see a man standing on a cart. He was speaking, and as the little boy hurried up, he heard him say, "I think we will all agree that we are wonderfully lucky and ought to be very thankful people. Also, I'm proud of the way we fought that fire. But all our efforts would have been useless if we had not had warning in time. So I want to give three cheers now for the boy who saw the fire while it was still far off and saved the town—Peter Rawdon!"

While the cheers rang out deafeningly, someone caught Peter and swung him up onto the cart, basket and all. It gave him a queer, dizzy feeling to be way up there looking down over all those laughing, friendly faces, but Peter was too concerned to be frightened or even embarrassed. A dreadful mistake had to be put right, and as soon as he could make himself heard he began to speak in an eager, excited little voice.

"I didn't save the town at all," he explained earnestly. "I was sound asleep. It was Bounce and Miss Gibbs who found out about the fire and thumped their pan until they woke me up. And then I forgot them and left them behind. But they weren't hurt after all. See, here they are!" And he lifted up the basket proudly.

For a moment there was an astonished silence. Then the cheering broke out louder than ever. "I think," cried the same man above the laughter and applause, "that we ought to give three cheers for Bounce and Miss Gibbs, but I wish we could show our gratitude in some more solid way. What do you say, Peter—would you like them to have a gold medal each or new collars? What would they like best?"

"I think," cried Peter, almost stammering in his excitement, "I think they would like best of all to be allowed to run about everywhere as they used to do, and I wish no one would ever shoot at them again, even if they do eat the young lettuce and turnips. Do you think they could?"

"Of course they shall!" cried the crowd, and Peter's mother, hugging him close a few moments later, whispered in his ear, "They may eat every vegetable I own, and I'll never say another word."

That very day the bunnies were given their freedom, and before long were the two best known and most petted members of the town. They still wrought havoc in the vegetable gardens, but whenever anyone felt inclined to be cross with them, even for a moment, he remembered how many, many more vegetables would have been lost—and how much else besides—if it had not been for Bounce and Miss Gibbs.

* * * * *

"Bounce and Miss Gibbs," by Eleanor Stimson Brooks. Published February 1918 in St. Nicholas. Eleanor Stimson Brooks wrote during the first few decades of the twentieth century.

SEVEN LITTLE FEATHERS

Lena Benthin
as told to Linda Franklin

Why in the world was the barn swallow so determined to get inside her house? Finally, just to find out, she let it in.

* * * * *

Yea, the sparrow hath found an house, and the swallow
a nest for herself, where she may lay her young
—Psalm 84:3, KJV.

The setting for this story is the little town of Irrigon, Oregon, where my Aunt Lena and Uncle Ed were raising their family in the 1960s. I remember Auntie's house—a friendly, simple farmhouse out on the open prairie. Although no one could ever explain scientifically the reason for this swallow's actions, I believe she understood my aunt's heart need at this particular time in her life. To Aunt Lena, the great out-of-doors, its Creator, her family, the farmyard animals, and wild creatures were her life. Allowing a swallow into her house was as natural to my aunt as adopting a homeless, three-legged dog. She effortlessly adapted her life to the needs of those she loved, and her home was claimed as often by animals in need as by her own family.

Once, when she was feeling so ill that she had to rest, Lena took time to write about a special little swallow who made herself at home until she was well once again.

* * * * *

The first week of June I see a few barn swallows flying around in the yard at evening time. One leaves the others and flutters in front of the glass in the door. Then they all fly to the backside of the house, flitting here and there, searching the patio for a place to rest.

One particular swallow comes back and hovers in front of me repeatedly as if to divert my attention from the dishes I am trying to wash in spite of my illness. She hangs on to the metal rim of the window then flies back to the storm door and back to my window. I smile at her antics as I struggle to finish the dishes. I just have not felt well today. In fact, I haven't been feeling well for several days.

The next day is Saturday. When I come in from doing the chores, I find the little swallow fighting the storm door ferociously, as if attacking an enemy. There is blood on the door. I must do something to relieve her anxiety. I leave the storm door open and then open the screened kitchen window too. She flies quickly onto the porch, sits on the frame of the door, and begins to sing. Soon she is  fighting the pane of glass in the back door, obviously wanting to come into the house. I am curious, but more concerned for her safety for she is now leaving blood on the window of the door.

When I finally open the door, she doesn't hesitate to enter, even with me still standing there. I sit down, thankful to take a little rest. I watch her as she inspects the living room six times, flitting through the kitchen and the hallway, hanging precariously on the door casings to rest. Her flight is graceful and skillful; she stops just short of the windows, obviously familiar with the illusions of glass. She sits on top of a door and begins to sing to me. The song wraps around me like a restful breeze. I begin to relax. It seems to me that I feel better for having stopped to listen.

She chooses the living room as her favorite place. Soon she is preening her feathers, stretching her legs out sideways, displaying the full spread of her lovely wings from a curtain rod. She stays in the house all day. About nine in the evening, she flies away, leaving me to wonder where she will sleep.

On Sunday she returns, singing joyfully to be back. I sit and watch her every move and listen to every sweet note. When she first returns, she is very noisy, excitedly telling me where she was and what she did during the night. We have friends visiting with us for Sunday dinner. When the swallow comes flitting through the house from a visit outdoors, our guests give us a strange look.

"Oh, that's Sarah," I say as I bring in a salad fresh from the garden.

They are used to seeing all kinds of animals come to our house for help, so, whatever else they may be thinking, they say, "Isn't that cute?" Comments are made as to where she must have come from. "Maybe she's someone's pet," one says. "Maybe she is ill," says another. They leave, and as I clean up, I am left to wonder why it is that Sarah insists on visiting our house.

Monday Sarah is playing with the drapery rod. Spying something on her beak, I get up in spite of my tiredness and take a closer look. I quickly realize that someone must lay down the law.

"Is that mud on your beak? Oh, no! You're not going to build a nest on that rod. No, you're not!" Sarah flutters around my head a couple of times, perches on the door, throws her mud on the floor, and leaves. *A bird tantrum?* I wonder. *She certainly didn't sing to me.*

Tuesday Sarah returns, having obviously forgiven me. She seems to have such fun—as if she loves us. She's so contented. I am still not feeling well, and as I lay on the couch Sarah hovers over me three times as if asking, "Are you all right?" It is so very hot I can hardly function today. Sarah's wings create a cool breeze over me. I relax and feel as if a rest might do me good. As if sensing that I am not up to mud, she leaves it outside. The last thing I remember before my eyes close peacefully are her two bright eyes looking at me. She watches over me as I rest and chirps when I awaken.

Wednesday she again flies in and out, talks and sings. No mud! At ten after nine, Sarah sings her good-night song, then with a few special chirps directed at me, she flies out into the night.

On Thursday we go into town, leaving her outdoors and the door shut. When we return in the evening, Sarah is waiting and stays inside with us until nine-thirty at which time she repeats the identical song she sang last night and leaves. I know, now, what she is saying. "Good night! Glad you are feeling a little better! See you tomorrow!"

Uh-oh! On Friday here she comes with a beak full of mud. I argue with myself, weighing the blood on the door against the mud in her beak. We have a staring contest through the window in the door. I try to remain firm. Sarah looks directly into my eyes. She wins. When I finally open the door, she goes directly to the rod above the curtain and lays a daub of mud there. In return trips, she lays daubs of mud here and there throughout the house, and I begin having second thoughts. *Maybe I am feeling a little better, but I am just not up to this mess.* I shake my head and sigh.

As if to read my mind, she stops her messing, sits on the top of the door again, and begins preening herself, showing me how beautiful she is and how privileged I am to have her as a guest. She cleans her feathers, stretches her wings and legs, moving swiftly, expertly. Sarah is truly beautiful. She has captivated me with her graceful flight, her gorgeous markings and color, and her cheerful attitude. Again, she chatters happily and sings to me. At nine-thirty in the evening, she chirps her now familiar farewell address and swoops out into the darkness.

On Saturday she flits in and out all day, looking over the house and choosing the drapery rod nearest the dining table, where the majority of our activity as a family takes place. She stays much longer tonight. It is dark in the living room, and I need to turn on the light. She leaves her perch on the door, flies around the living room, spies a couple of flies on the ceiling, and takes care of them for me.

Though I am still not strong, I have a chore or two in the kitchen. Sarah circles my head twice and goes back to her perch on the door. At a quarter to ten, just about the time I decide that she must be spending the night, she chirps her "good-night greeting" and flies away.

At six-thirty on Sunday morning Sarah hauls in her first serious load of mud. She is in a working mood today. Although it doesn't look as if she is accomplishing much, she is still working at ten after ten at night. I turn out the lights. In the darkness I hear her sing her good-night song. I can dimly see her as she circles the living room twice and is gone.

Monday morning she is hard at it again by six-thirty, working steadily, packing mud until nine that evening at which time she reexamines her work, sings her good-night song, and chirps an additional message directed at me as if to say, "Don't be sad; I'll be back tomorrow, but I might sleep in a while. It's been a hard day's work!" Then she flies out into the warm summer night.

On Tuesday Sarah sleeps in. She doesn't start putting the "siding" on her nest until seven in the morning. All day long she works on the inside of her nest which is now about an inch and half high. She rolls around in the nest, removing a little mud here and there, muttering to herself as she works. She is particular in her building requirements. At nine, she does her last inspection, sings us her good-night song, and leaves.

Wednesday morning I hear Sarah before I see her. She sits outside the window singing to me, reminding me that she is ready to begin. At a quarter after seven, when I open the door, she darts into the living room. I know she is anxious to begin her work, but before she starts, she sits on the drapery rod and sings to me. I appreciate her visit, as I am still not strong. I am happy to rest a while, watching her glide around the room. Resting on the curtain rod, Sarah tips her head from side to side, chirping at me as if inquiring about my health, then she goes to work.

How our family is learning to love this little artist! This evening the children sit with me for a while on the couch, and together we watch as Sarah puts the finishing touches on her nest. She swoops outside to bring in some fine, dry grass with which to line it and then scoops out the rejects, watching them fall onto the carpet below. At a quarter to nine, she sings us her goodbye song and darts quickly out the door.

On Thursday I go to town early, and Sarah is waiting for me on the doorsill when I return. It is very hot so I leave the door wide open. She sits quietly on her nest all day and says goodbye at eight-forty.

Sarah flies to our bedroom window at six-thirty Friday morning, singing and talking. She comes in once this morning, sits a while, and leaves again. She returns in the afternoon bringing bits of straw with each trip, then turns around and around in her nest several times making certain of its comfort. Our two daughters come at different times this evening to visit. In the process of our visiting, I somehow miss the farewell song. Perhaps she didn't bother to sing it to me tonight, knowing I was busy. Or maybe she sensed my health was beginning to improve and that I didn't need her song as desperately as before.

Saturday, it seems Sarah must have known we are leaving early this morning for the Carper family reunion in Washington. She does not come inside. My husband, Ed, stays home. He goes to work in Boardman and doesn't see her for the rest of the day, even at supper-time.

Sunday, Sarah is an early bird, obviously happy that we are all home again—singing and talking to us either at the window or the door or sitting on the rim of the finished nest. She is so cheerful and beautiful I find myself wishing for an artist's talent so that I could capture her joy and beauty on paper.

I catch my breath at her indescribable beauty as she hovers over the hallway entrance when I emerge from the bedroom. She flies to the kitchen entrance and repeats her fabulous aerial ballet for my daughter, Bonnie, then darts outside.

On Monday, we must go to Heppner for business. I am feeling much better now. It is hot, and we leave the kitchen door open for ventilation. At three in the afternoon when we return, Sarah is not there to sing to us. At six-thirty in the evening, I go out to check on the cattle and see a noxious weed called dodder. While I am pulling it, a swallow comes within a few feet of my head, chattering a steady stream of very anxious swallow talk. I try to see if this is our swallow, but I cannot tell. I wonder if this is ours or if I am hearing what is happening to ours. I return home and listen intently for Sarah, but she does not return.

Tuesday dawns with a painful silence. I listen and watch for her. Yesterday I began feeling much better and even had some energy, for the first time in weeks, so I start a load of laundry. Although I have more physical strength, something aches deep inside, an emotional void that needs filling. A tiny feather on the washing machine reminds me of why I am feeling so empty. All day I listen subconsciously for Sarah's return while performing my daily chores. Outside I find six more feathers on the ground. It is becoming clear to me that our little friend will not be returning.

After Sarah has been gone for a week, I carefully remove her nest from the curtain rod and place it gently in a small birdcage. I arrange the seven little feathers in Sarah's nest, hoping the arrangement would be pleasing to my little friend. I clean up the little mud spots where she had tested other building sites on three other curtain rods and a battery-operated clock before she chose her nesting place.

At first, only sadness accompanies the memory of this great loss. We all miss Sarah terribly. After a while, the precious memory becomes bittersweet. Why did little Sarah choose our house? Why did she trust us so completely? Suddenly the thought comes to me: *What if she had hatched her babies in our house—feeding them every day, teaching them to fly in our living room?* My mind's eye easily captures that scenario: *What if all of Sarah's aerial offspring returned every year to our house instead of Capistrano and were as determined as their mother had been to raise a family in our living room?*

I take the little nest in my hands, fondle the seven dainty, dark feathers and, finally, I can smile through my tears.

* * * *

"Seven Little Feathers," by Lena Benthin, as told to Linda Franklin. Printed by permission of the author. Linda Franklin lives and writes from her home in Chetwynd, British Columbia. She has made a specialty of stories depicting the interrelationship of humans and birds.

The Battle of the Buffaloes

Alexander Majors

What a sight it must have been to see the vast buffalo herds in their heyday, when some seventy million roamed the Great Plains! Today, the few remaining great beasts seem so tame it's almost like looking at over-grown cows.

This is why the following account of a duel between two great buffalo bulls by Alexander Majors (cofounder of the legendary Pony Express) is such a treasure.

* * * * *

It was the afternoon of a day in early summer in 1859, when we found ourselves drifting in a boat down the Missouri. The morning broke with a drizzling rain, out of a night that had been tempestuous, with a fierce gale, heavy thunder, and unusually terrific lightning. Gradually the rain stopped, and we had gone but a short distance when the clouds broke away, the sun shone forth, and the earth appeared glistening with a new beauty. Ahead of us appeared, high up on the bluffs, a clump of trees and bushes.

As we drew near, a sudden caprice seized us, and shooting our boat up on the shelving bank, we secured it and then climbed the steep embankment. We intended to knock around in the brush a little while and then resume our trip. A fine specimen of an eagle caught our eye, perched high up on the dead bough of a tree.

Moving around to get a good position to pick him off with my rifle, so that his body would not be turned, I caught sight through an opening of the trees of an immense herd of buffaloes, browsing and moving slowly in our direction. We moved forward a little to get a better view of the herd, when the eagle, unaware to us, spread his pinions, and when we looked again for him he was soaring at a safe distance from our rifles.

We were on the leeward side of the herd and among the trees, and so safe from discovery if we took ordinary precautions. It was a fine spectacle which they presented, and what was more, we were in just the mood to watch them. The land was covered for many acres with minute undulations of dark brown shoulders slowly drifting toward us. We could hear the rasping sound which innumerable mouths made chopping the crisp grass. As we looked, our ears caught a low, faint, rhythmical sound, borne to us from afar.

We listened intently. The sound grew more distinct, until we could recognize the tread of another herd of buffaloes coming from an opposite direction.

We skulked low through the undergrowth and came to the edge of the wooded patch just in time to see the vanguard of this new herd surmounting a hill. The herd was evidently spending its force, having already run for miles. It came with a lessening speed, until it settled down to a comfortable walk.

About the same time the two herds discovered each other. Our herd was at first a little startled, but after a brief inspection of the approaching mass, the work of clipping the grass of the prairies was resumed. The fresh arrivals came to a standstill, and gazed at the thousands of their fellows, who evidently had preempted their grazing grounds. Apparently, they reached the conclusion that that region was common property, for they soon lowered their heads and began to shave the face of the earth of its green growth.

The space separating the herds slowly lessened. The outermost fringes touched but a short distance from our point of observation. It was not like the fringes of a lady's dress coming in contact with the lace drapery of a window, I can assure you. Nothing so soft and sibilant as that. It was more like the fringes of freight engines coming in contact with each other when they approach with some momentum on the same track.

Two powerful bulls unwittingly found themselves in close proximity to each other, coming from opposite herds. Suddenly shooting up from the sides of the one whose herd was on the ground first, flumes of dirt made graceful curves in the air. They were the signals for hostilities to commence. The hooves of the powerful beast were assisted by his small horns, which dug the sod and tossed clumps into the air, some settling in his shaggy mane.

These belligerent demonstrations were responded to in quite as defiant a fashion by the late arrival. He, too, was an enormous affair. We noticed his unusual proportions of head. But his shoulders, with its great mane, were worth displaying to excite admiration and awe at their possibilities, if they could do nothing more.

Unquestionably the two fellows regarded themselves as representative of their different herds, the one first on the ground viewing the other as an interloper, and he in his turn looking upon the former as reigning merely because no one had the spirit to contest his supremacy and show him where he belonged. They sidled up near each other, their heads all the while kept low to the ground, and their eyes red with anger and rolling in fierce fury. This display of the preliminaries of battle drew the attention of an increasing number from each herd. At first they would look up, then recommence their eating, and then direct their attention more intensely as the combatants began to measure their strength more closely. And when the fight was on they became quite absorbed in the varying fortunes of the struggle.

At last the two huge fellows, after a good deal of circumlocution, made the grand rush. (I reckon it would be your everlasting fortune if one of you college fellows who play football had the force to make the great rush which either one of these animals presented.) The collision was straight and square. A crash of horns, a heavy, dull thud of heads. We thought surely the skull of one or the other, or possibly both, was crushed in. But evidently they were not even hurt.

Didn't they push then? Well, I guess they did. The force would have shoved an old-fashioned barn from its foundations. The muscles swelled up on the thighs, the hoofs sank into the earth, but they were evenly matched.

For a moment there was a mutual cessation of hostilities in order to regain breath. Then they came together with a more resounding crash than before. Instantly we perceived that the meeting of the heads was not square. The new champion had the best position. Like a flash he recognized it and redoubled his efforts to take full advantage of it. The other appeared to quadruple his efforts to maintain himself in position, and his muscles bulged out, but his antagonist made a sudden move which wrenched his head still farther off the line, and he went down on his knees. That settled the contest, for his enemy was upon him before he could recover. He was thrown aside, and his flank raked by several ugly upward thrusts of his foe, which left him torn and bruised, all in a heap. As quick as he could get on his feet he limped, crestfallen, away.

The victorious fellow lashed his small tail, tossed his head, and moved in all the pride of his contest up and down through the ranks of his adversary's herd. How exultant he was! We took it to be rank impudence, and though he had exhibited some heroic qualities of strength and daring, it displeased us to see him take on so many airs on account of his victory.

But his conquest of the field was not yet entirely complete. As he strode proudly along, his progress was stopped by a loud snort, and looking aside, he saw a fresh challenge. There, standing out in full view, was another bull, a monster of a fellow belonging to his late enemy's herd. He pawed the earth with great strokes and sent rockets of turf curving high in air, some of which sifted its fine soil down upon the nose of the victor.

As we looked at this new challenger and took in his immense form, we chuckled with the assurance that the haughty fellow would now have some decent humility imposed upon him. The conqueror himself must have been impressed with the formidableness of his new antagonist, for there was a change in his demeanor at once. Of course, according to a well-established buffalo code, he could do nothing but accept the challenge.

Space was cleared as the two monsters went through their gyrations, their tossings of earth, their lashings of tail, their snorts and their low bellows. This appeared to them a more serious contest than the former, if we could judge from the length of the introductory part. They took more time before they settled down to business. We were of the opinion that the delay was caused by the champion, who resorted to small arts to prolong the preliminaries. We watched it all with the most excited interest. It had all the thrilling features of a Spanish bullfight without the latter's degradation of man. Here was the level of nature. Here the true buffalo instincts with their native temperament were exhibiting themselves in the most emphatic and vigorous fashion. It was the buffalo's trial of nerve, strength, and skill. Numberless as must have been these tournaments in which the champions of different herds met to decide which was superior, in the long ages during which the buffalo kingdom reigned supreme over the vast western prairies of the United States, yet few had ever been witnessed by man. We were looking upon a spectacle rare to human eyes, and I confess that I was never more excited than when this last trial reached its climax. It was a question now whether the champion should still retain his position. It hurts one more when he thinks of losing what he has seized than when he thinks of failing to grasp that which he has never possessed. Undoubtedly both of these animals had this same feeling, for as we looked at this latest arrival we about concluded that he was the real leader, and not the other that limped away vanquished.

While these and other thoughts were passing through our minds, the two mighty contestants squared and made a tremendous plunge for each other. What a shock was that! What a report rolled on the air! The earth fairly shook with the terrific concussion of buffalo brains, and both burly fellows went down on their knees. Both, too, were on their feet the same instant, and locked horns with the same swiftness and skill, and each bore down on the other with all the power he could summon. The cords stood out like great ropes on their necks; the muscles on thighs and hips rose like huge welts. We were quite near these fellows and could see the roll of the blood-red fiery eyes. They braced and shoved with perfectly terrible force. The froth began to drip in long strings from their mouths. The erstwhile victor slipped with one hind foot slightly. His antagonist felt it and instantly swung a couple of inches forward, which raised the unfortunate buffalo's back, and we expected every instant that he would go down. But he had a firm hold, and he swung his antagonist back to his former position, where they were both held panting, their tongues lolling out.

There was a slight pause for breath, then the contest was renewed. Deep into the new sod their hoofs sank, neither getting the advantage of the other. Like a crack of a tree broken asunder came a report on the air, and one of the legs of the first fighter sank into the earth. The other buffalo thought he saw his chance and made a furious lunge toward his opponent. The earth trembled beneath us. The monsters there fighting began to reel. We beheld an awful rent in the sod. For an instant the ground swayed, then nearly an acre dropped out of sight!

We started back with horror, then becoming reassured, we slowly approached the brink of the new precipice and looked over. This battle of the buffaloes had been fought near the edge of this high bluff. Their great weight—each was over a ton—and their tremendous struggles had loosened the fibers which kept the upper part of the bluff together, and the foundations having been undermined by the current, all were precipitated into the river far below.

As we gazed downward, we detected two moving masses quite a distance apart, and soon the shaggy fronts of these buffaloes were seen. One got into the current of the river and was swept downstream. The other soon was caught by the tides and swept on toward his foe. Possibly they resumed the contest when, after gaining a good footing farther down the banks of the Missouri, they were fully rested.

But more probably, if they were sensible animals, and in some respects buffaloes have good sense, they concluded after such a providential interference in their terrific fight that they should live together in fraternal amity. So, no doubt, on the lower waters of the Missouri two splendid buffaloes have been seen by later hunters paying each other mutual respect and standing on a perfect equality as chief leaders of a great herd.

* * * * *

"The Battle of the Buffaloes," by Alexander Majors. Included in Majors's book, Seventy Years on the Frontier *(Chicago: Rand McNally, 1893). Alexander Majors (1814–1900) was a principal figure in the settling of the West. He, William H. Russell, and William B. Waddell for a time dominated transportation in the West and Southwest. The three men organized the Pony Express in 1860.*

THE LORD OF LACKAWAXEN CREEK

Zane Grey

What is it about fishing that summons the eternal child in each of us? That thrill of anticipation—Today, I'll land a big one!

Whatever that call may be, thirty-four million Americans respond to it every year. This true story, written by Zane Grey in 1909 at the very beginning of his illustrious career, has become, over time, perhaps the most famed and beloved fishing story ever written.

Our Lord, who Himself loved to fish, would have empathized with both the fisherman who yearned to catch the big one, and the big one who had no intention of ever being caught.

* * * * *

Winding among the Blue Hills of Pennsylvania, there is a swift amber stream that the Indians named *Lack-a-wax-en*. The literal translation no one seems to know, but it must mean, in mystical and imaginative Delaware, "the brown water that turns and whispers and tumbles." It is a little river hidden away under gray cliffs and hills black with ragged pines. It is full of mossy stones and rapid ripples.

All its tributaries, dashing white-sheeted over ferny cliffs, wine-brown where the whirling pools suck the stain from the hemlock root, harbor the speckled trout. Wise in their generation, the black and red-spotted little beauties keep to their brooks; for farther down, below the rush and fall, a newcomer is lord of the stream. He is an archenemy, a scorner of beauty and blood, the wolf-jawed, red-eyed, bronze-backed black bass.

A mile or more from its mouth, the Lackawaxen leaves the shelter of the hills and seeks the open sunlight and slows down to widen into long lanes that glide reluctantly over the few last re-straining barriers to the Delaware. In a curve between two of these level lanes, there is a place where barefoot boys wade and fish for chubs and bask on the big boulders like turtles. It is a famous hole of chubs and bright-sided shiners and sunfish. And, perhaps because it is so known and so shallow, so open to the sky, few fishermen ever learned that in its secret stony caverns hid a great golden-bronze treasure of a bass.

In vain had many a flimsy feathered hook been flung over his lair by fly casters and whisked gracefully across the gliding surface of his pool. In vain had many a shiny spoon and pearly minnow reflected sun glints through the watery windows of his home. In vain had many a hellgrammite and frog and grasshopper been dropped in front of his broad nose.

Chance plays the star part in a fisherman's luck. One still, cloudy day, when the pool glanced dark under a leaden sky, I saw a wave that reminded me of the wake of a rolling tarpon; then followed an angry swirl, the skitter of a frantically leaping chub, and a splash that ended with a sound like the deep chung of water sharply turned by an oar.

Big bass choose strange hiding places. They should be looked for in just such holes and rifts and shallows as will cover their backs. But to corral a six-pounder in the boys' swimming hole was a circumstance to temper a fisherman's vanity with experience.

Thrillingly conscious of the possibilities of this pool, I studied it thoughtfully. It was a wide, shallow bend in the stream, with dark channels between submerged rocks, suggestive of underlying shelves. It had a current, too, not noticeable at first glance. And this pool looked at long and carefully, colored by the certainty of its guardian, took on an aspect most alluring to an angler's spirit. It had changed from a pond girt by stony banks, to a foam-flecked running stream— clear, yet hiding its secrets; shallow, yet full of labyrinthine watercourses. It presented problems, which difficult as they were, faded in a breath before a fisherman's optimism.

I tested my leader, changed the small hook for a large one, and selecting a white shiner fully six inches long, I lightly hooked it through the side of the upper lip. A sensation never outgrown since boyhood, a familiar mingling of strange fear and joyous anticipation, made me stoop low and tread the slippery stones as if I were a stalking Indian. I knew that a glimpse of me or a faint vibration under the water, or an unnatural ripple on its surface would be fatal to my enterprise.

I swung the lively minnow and instinctively dropped it with a splash over a dark space between two yellow sunken stones. Out of the amber depths started a broad bar of bronze, rose and flashed into gold. A little dimpling eddying circle, most fascinating of all watery forms, appeared round where the minnow had sunk. The golden moving flash went down and vanished in the greenish gloom like a tiger stealing into a jungle. The line trembled, slowly swept out and straightened. How fraught that instant with a wild yet waiting suspense, with a thrill potent and blissful!

Did the fisherman ever live who could wait in such a moment? My arms twitched involuntarily. Then I struck hard, but not half hard enough. The bass leaped out of a flying splash, shook himself in a tussle plainly audible, and slung the hook back at me like a bullet.

In such moments one never sees the fish distinctly; excitement deranges the vision, and the picture, though impressive, is dim and dreamlike. But a blind man would have known this bass to be enormous, for when he fell he cut the water like a heavy stone.

The best aspect of fishing is that a mild philosophy attends even the greatest misfortunes. It is a delusion peculiar to fishermen, and I went on my way upstream, cheerfully, as one who minded not at all an incident of angling practice; spiritedly, as one who had seen many a big bass go by the board. I found myself thinking about my two brothers, Cedar and Reddy for short, both anglers of long standing and some reputation. It was a sore point with me and a stock subject for endless disputes that they could never appreciate my superiority as a fisherman. Brothers are singularly prone to such points of view. So when I thought of them, I felt the incipient stirring of a mighty plot. It occurred to me that the iron-mouthed old bass, impregnable of jaw as well as of stronghold, might be made to serve a turn. And all the afternoon the thing grew and grew in my mind.

Luck otherwise favored me, and I took home a fair string of fish. I remarked to my brothers that the conditions for fishing the stream were favorable. Thereafter, morning after morning, my eyes sought the heavens, appealing for a cloudy day. At last one came, and I invited Reddy to go with me. With childish pleasure that would have caused weakness in any but an unscrupulous villain, he eagerly accepted. He looked over a great assortment of tackle and finally selected a five-ounce Leonard bait rod carrying a light reel and fine line. When I thought of what would happen if Reddy hooked that powerful bass, an unholy glee fastened upon my soul.

We never started out that way together, swinging rods and pails, but old associations were awakened. We called up the time when we had left the imprints of bare feet on the country roads; we lived over many a boyhood adventure by a running stream. And at last we wound up on the never threadbare question as to the merit and use of tackle.

"I always claim," said Reddy, "that a fisherman should choose tackle for a day's work after the fashion of a hunter choosing his gun. A hunter knows what kind of game he's after and takes a small or large caliber gun accordingly. Of course a fisherman has more rods than there are calibers of guns, but the rule holds. Now today I have brought this light rod and thin line because I don't need weight. I don't see why you've brought that heavy rod. Even a two-pound bass would be a great surprise up this stream."

"You're right," I replied, "but I sort of lean toward possibilities. Besides, I'm fond of this rod. You know I've caught a half dozen bass of five to six pounds with it. I wonder what you would do if you hooked a big one on your delicate rod."

"Do?" exclaimed my brother. "I'd have a fit! I might handle a big bass in deep water with this outfit, but here in this shallow stream with its rocks and holes, I couldn't. And that is the reason so few big bass are taken from the Delaware. We know they are there, great lusty fellows! Every day in season we hear some tale of woe from some fisherman: 'Hooked a big one—broke this—broke that—got under a stone.' That's why no five- or six-pound bass are taken from shallow, swift, rock-bedded streams on light tackle."

When we reached the pool, I sat down and began to fumble with my leader. How generously I let Reddy have the first cast! My iniquity carried me to the extreme of bidding him steal softly and stoop low. I saw a fat chub swinging in the air; I saw it alight to disappear in a churning commotion of water, and I heard Reddy's startled expression of surprise.

Hard upon his exclamation followed action of striking swiftness. A shrieking reel, willow wand of a rod wavering like a buggy whip in the wind, curving splashes around a foam-lashed swell, a crack of dry wood, a sound as of a banjo string snapping, a sharp splash, then a heavy sullen souse; these, with Reddy standing voiceless, eyes glaring on the broken rod and limp trailing line, were the essentials of the tragedy.

Somehow the joke did not ring true when Reddy waded ashore calm and self-contained, with only his burning eyes to show how deeply he felt. What he said to me in a quiet voice must not, owing to family pride, go on record. It most assuredly would not be an addition to the fish literature of the day.

But he never mentioned the incident to Cedar, which omission laid the way open for my further machinations. I realized now that I should have tried Cedar first. He was one of those white-duck-pants-on-a-dry-rock sort of a fisherman, anyway. And in due time I had him wading out toward the center of that pool.

I always experienced a painful sensation while watching Cedar cast. One moment he resembled Ajax defying the lightning and the next he looked like the fellow who stood on a monument, smiling at grief. Cedar's execution was wonderful. I have seen him cast a frog a mile—but the frog had left the hook. It was remarkable to see him catch his hat and terrifying to hear the language he used at such an ordinary angling event. It was not safe to be in his vicinity, but if this was unavoidable, the better course was to face him; because if you turned your back an instant, his flying hook would have a fiendish affinity for your trousers, and it was not beyond his powers to swing you kicking out over the stream. All of which, considering the frailties of human nature and of fishermen, could be forgiven; he had, however, one great fault impossible to overlook, and it was that he made more noise than a playful hippopotamus.

I hoped, despite all these things, that the big bass would rise to the occasion. He did rise. He must have recognized the situation of his life. He spread the waters of his shallow pool and accommodatingly hooked himself.

Cedar's next graceful move was to fall off the slippery stone on which he had been standing and to go out of sight. His hat floated downstream; the arched tip of his rod came up, then his arm, and his dripping shoulders and body. He yelled like a savage and pulled on the fish hard enough to turn a tuna in the air. The big bass leaped three times, made a long shoot with his black dorsal fin showing, and then, with a lunge, headed for some place remote from there. Cedar plowed after him, sending the water in sheets, and then he slipped, wildly swung his arms and fell again.

I was sinking to the ground, owing to unutterable and overpowering sensations of joy, when a yell and a commotion in the bushes heralded the appearance of Reddy.

"Hang on, Cedar! Hang on!" he cried and began an Indian war dance.

The few succeeding moments were somewhat blurred because of my excess of motion. When I returned to consciousness, Cedar was wading out with a hookless leader, a bloody shin, and a disposition utterly and irretrievably ruined.

"You put a job on me!" he roared.

Thereafter during the summer each of us made solitary and sneaking expeditions bent on the capture of the lord of the Lackawaxen. And somehow each would return to find the other two derisively speculating as to what caused his clouded brow. Leader on leader went to grace the rocks of the old bronze warrior's home. At length Cedar and Reddy gave up, leaving the pool to me. I fed more than one choice shiner to the bass, and more than once he sprang into the air to return my hook.

Summer and autumn passed; winter came to lock the Lackawaxen in icy fetters. I fished under Southern skies where lagoons and moss-shaded waters teemed with great and gamey fish, but I never forgot him. I knew that when the season rolled around, when a June sun warmed the cold spring-fed Lackawaxen, he would be waiting for me.

Who was it spoke of the fleeting of time? Obviously, he had never waited for the opening of the fishing season. At last the tedious time, like the water, flowed by. But then I found I had another long wait.

Brilliant June days without a cloud were a joy to live, but worthless for fishing. Through all that beautiful month I plodded up to the pool only to be unrewarded. Doubt began to assail me. Might not the ice, during the spring breakup, have scared him from the shallow hole? No. I felt that not even a rolling glacier could have moved him from his subterranean home.

Often as I reached the pool, I saw fishermen wading down the stream, and on these occasions I sat on the bank and lazily waited for the intruders to pass on. Once, the first time I saw them, I had an agonizing fear that one of the yellow-helmeted, khaki-coated anglers would hook my bass. The fear, of course, was groundless. The idea of that grand fish rising to take a feathery imitation of a bug or a lank dead bait had nothing in my experience to warrant its consideration. Small, lively bass, full of play, fond of chasing their golden shadows, and belligerent and hungry, were ready to fight and eat whatever swam into their ken. But a six-pound bass, slow to reach such weight in swift-running water, was old and wise and full of years. He did not feed often, and when he did he wanted a live fish big enough for a good mouthful. So, with these facts to soothe me, I rested my fears and got to look humorously at the invasions of the summer-hotel fishermen.

They came wading, slipping, splashing downstream, blowing like porpoises, slapping at the water with all kinds of artificial and dead bait. And they called to me in a humor inspired by my fishing garb and the rustic environment.

"Hey, Rube! Ketchin' any?"

I said the suckers were bitin' right pert.

"What d'you call this stream?"

I replied, giving the Indian name.

"Lack-a-what? Can't you whistle it? Lack-a-whacken? You mean Lack-a-fishin'. "

"Lack-a-rotten," joined in another.

"Do you live here?" questioned a third.

I said Yes.

"Why don't you move?" Whereupon they all laughed and pursued the noisy tenor of their way downstream, pitching their baits around.

"Say, fellows," I shouted after them, "are you training for the casting tournament in Madison Square Garden or do you think you're playing lacrosse?" The laugh that came back proved the joke on them and that it would be remembered as part of the glorious time they were having.

July brought misty, dark, lowering days. Not only did I find the old king at home on these days, but just as contemptuous of hooks and leaders as he had been the summer before. About the middle of the month he stopped giving me paralysis of the heart; that is to say, he quit rising to my tempting chums and shiners. So I left him alone to rest, to rust out hooks and grow less suspicious.

By the time August came, the desire to call on him again was well-nigh irresistible. But I waited, and fished the Delaware, and still waited. I would get him when the harvest moon was full. Like all the old mossbacked denizens of the shady holes, he would come out then for a last range over the feeding shoals. At length a morning broke humid and warm, almost dark as twilight, with little gusts of fine rain. Of all days this was the day! I chose a stiff rod, a heavy silk line, a stout brown leader, and a large hook. From my bait box I took two five-inch red catfish, the little "stone-rollers" of the Delaware, and several long shiners. Thus equipped, I sallied forth.

The walk up the tow path, along the canal with its rushes and sedges, across the meadows white with late-blooming daisies, lost nothing because of its familiarity. When I reached the pool, I saw in the low water near shore several small bass scouting among the schools of minnows. I did not want these pugnacious fellows to kill my bait; so, procuring a hellgrammite from under a stone, I put it on my hook and promptly caught two of them, and gave the other a scare he would not soon forget.

I decided to try the bass with one of his favorite shiners. With this trailing in the water, I silently waded out, making not so much as a ripple. The old familiar oppression weighed on my breast; the old throbbing boyish excitement tingled through my blood. I made a long cast and dropped the shiner lightly. It went under and then came up to swim about on the surface. This was a sign that made my heart leap. Then the water bulged, and a black bar shot across the middle of the long shiner. He went down out of sight, the last gleams of his divided brightness fading slowly. I did not need to see the little shower of silver scales floating up to know that the black bar had been the rounded nose of the old bass and that he had taken the shiner across the middle. I struck hard, and my hook came whistling at me. I had scored a clean miss.

I waded ashore very carefully, sat down on a stone by my bait pail, and meditated. Would he rise again? I had never known him to do so twice in one day. But then there had never been occasion. I thought of the stone-rollers and thrilled with certainty. Whatever he might resist, he could not resist one of those little red catfish. Long ago, when he was only a three- or four-pounder roaming the deep eddies and swift rapids of the Delaware, before he had isolated himself to a peaceful old age in this quiet pool, he must have poked his nose under many a stone, with red eyes keen for one of those dainty morsels.

My excitation thrilled itself out to the calm assurance of the experienced fisherman. I firmly fastened on one of the catfish and stole out into the pool. I waded farther than ever before; I was careful but confident. Then I saw the two flat rocks dimly shining. The water was dark as it rippled by, gurgling softly; it gleamed with lengthening shadows and glints of amber.

I swung the catfish. A dull flash of sunshine seemed to come up to meet him. The water swirled and broke with a splash. The broad black head of the bass just skimmed the surface; his jaws opened wide to take in the bait; he turned and flapped a huge spread tail on the water.

Then I struck with all the power the tackle would stand. I felt the hook catch solidly as if in a sunken log. Swift as flashing light the bass leaped. The drops of water hissed and the leader whizzed. But the hook held. I let out one exultant yell. He did not leap again. He dashed to the right, then the left, in bursts of surprising speed. I had hardly warmed to the work when he settled down and made for the dark channel between the yellow rocks. My triumph was to be short-lived. Where was the beautiful spectacular surface fight I expected of him? Cunning old monarch! He laid his great weight dead on the line and lunged for his sunken throne. I held him with a grim surety of the impossibility of stopping him. How I longed for deep, open water! The rod bent, the line strained and stretched. I removed my thumb and the reel sang one short shrill song. Then the bass was as still as the rock under which he had gone.

I had never dislodged a big bass from under a stone, and I saw herein further defeat; but I persevered, wading to different angles, and working all the tricks of the trade. I could not drag the fish out, nor pull the hook loose. I sat down on a stone and patiently waited for a long time, hoping he would come out of his own accord.

As a final resort I waded out. The water rose to my waist, then to my shoulders, my chin, and all but covered my raised face. When I reached the stone under which he had planted himself, I stood in water about four feet deep. I saw my leader, and tugged upon it, and kicked under the stone, all to no good.

Then I calculated I had a chance to dislodge him if I could get my arm under the shelf. So I went—hat, rod, and all. The current was just swift enough to lift my feet, making my task most difficult. At the third trial I got my hand on a sharp corner of stone and held fast. I ran my right hand along the leader, under the projecting slab of rock, till I touched the bass. I tried to get hold of him, but had to rise for air.

I dove again. The space was narrow, so narrow that I wondered how so large a fish could have gotten there. He had gone under sidewise, turned, and wedged his dorsal fin, fixing himself as solidly as the rock itself. I pulled frantically till I feared I would break the leader.

When I floundered up to breathe again, the thought occurred to me that I could rip him with my knife and, by taking the life out of him, loosen the powerful fin so he could be dragged out. Still, much as I wanted him, I could not do that. I resolved to make one more fair attempt. In a quick determined plunge, I secured a more favorable hold for my left hand and reached under with my right. I felt his whole long length, and I could not force a finger behind him anywhere. The gill toward me was shut tight like a trapdoor. But I got a thumb and forefinger fastened to his lip. I tugged till a severe cramp numbed my hand; I saw red and my head whirled; a noise roared in my ears. I stayed until one more second would have made me a drowning man, then rose gasping and choking.

I broke off the leader close to the stone and waded ashore. I looked back at the pool, faintly circled by widening ripples. What a great hole and what a grand fish! I was glad I did not get him and knew I would never again disturb his peace.

So I took my rod and pail and the two little bass, and brushed the meadow daisies, and threaded the familiar green-lined tow path toward home.

* * * * *

"The Lord of Lackawaxen Creek," by Zane Grey. Reprinted by permission of Zane Grey, Inc. Zane Grey (1872–1939) was born in Zanesville, Ohio. He was the highest-selling and highest-paid author in the world during the first half of the twentieth century. He is considered to be the father of the western novel and the last chronicler of the frontier to write while the frontier still existed. He was also one of the leading nature writers of his time.

RAGGYLUG

Ernest Thompson Seton

Few wild animals face tougher survival odds than the rabbit. Naturalist Ernest Thompson Seton remembers one particular rabbit that had more close calls than one would believe possible. He named him "Raggylug."

* * * * *

Raggylug, or Rag, was the name of a young cottontail rabbit. It was given him from his torn and ragged ear, a life mark that he got in his first adventure. He lived with his mother in Olifant's swamp, where I made their acquaintance and gathered, in a hundred different ways, the little bits of proof and scraps of truth that at length enabled me to write this history.

Those who do not know the animals well may think I have humanized them, but those who have lived so near them as to know somewhat of their ways and their minds will not think so.

Truly rabbits have no speech as we understand it, but they have a way of conveying ideas by a system of sounds, signs, scents, whisker touches, movements, and examples that answer the purpose of speech.

I

The rank swamp grass bent over and concealed the snug nest where Raggylug's mother had hidden him. She had partly covered him with some of the bedding, and, as always, she taught him to lie low and make no sound, whatever happened. Though tucked in bed, he was wide awake, and his bright eyes were taking in that part of his little green world that was straight above. A blue jay and a red squirrel, two notorious thieves, were loudly berating each other for stealing, and at one time Rag's home bush was the center of their fight; a yellow warbler caught a blue butterfly but six inches from his nose; and a scarlet-and-black ladybug, serenely waving her knobbed feelers, took a long walk up one grass blade, down another, and across the nest and over Rag's face—and yet he never moved nor even winked.

After a while he heard a strange rustling of the leaves in the near thicket. It was an odd, continuous sound, and though it went this way and that way and came ever nearer, there was no patter of feet with it. Rag had lived his whole life in the swamp (he was three weeks old) and yet had never heard anything like this. Of course his curiosity was greatly aroused. His mother had cautioned him to lie low, but that was understood to be in case of danger, and this strange sound without footfalls could not be anything to fear.

The low rasping went past close at hand, then to the right, then back, and seemed to be going away. Rag felt he knew what he was about; he wasn't a baby; it was his duty to learn what it was. He slowly raised his roly-poly body on his short fluffy legs, lifted his little round head above the covering of his nest, and peeped out into the woods. The sound ceased as soon as he moved. He saw nothing, so took one step forward to a clear view and instantly found himself face to face with an enormous black serpent.

He cried out in mortal terror as the monster darted at him. With all the strength of his tiny limbs he tried to run. But in a flash the snake had him by one ear and whipped around him with his coils to gloat over the helpless little baby bunny he had secured for dinner. . . .

But bounding through the woods straight as an arrow came his mother. No longer a shy, helpless little Molly Cottontail, ready to fly from a shadow; the mother's love was strong in her. The cry of her baby filled her with the courage of a hero, and—hop, she went over that horrible reptile. Whack, she struck down at him with her sharp hind claws as she passed, giving him such a stinging blow that he squirmed with pain and hissed with anger. . . .

Molly came leaping again and again and struck harder and fiercer, until the loathsome reptile let go the little one's ear and tried to bite the old one as she leaped over. But all he got was a mouthful of wool each time, and Molly's fierce blows began to tell, as long bloody rips were torn in the black snake's scaly armor.

Things were now looking bad for the snake; and bracing himself for the next charge, he lost his tight hold on baby bunny, who at once wriggled out of the coils and away into the underbrush, breathless and terribly frightened, but unhurt save that his left ear was much torn by the teeth of that dreadful serpent.

Molly had now gained all she wanted. She had no notion of fighting for glory or revenge. Away she went into the woods, and the little one followed the shining beacon of her snow-white tail until she led him to a safe corner of the swamp.

II

Ole Olifant's swamp was a rough, brambly tract of second growth woods with a marshy pond and a stream through the middle. A few ragged remnants of the old forest still stood in it, and a few of the still older trunks were lying about as dead logs in the brushwood. The land about the pond was of the willow-grown sedgy kind that cats and horses avoid, but cattle do not fear. The drier zones were overgrown with briers and young trees. The outermost belt of all, that next to the fields, was of thrifty, gummy-trunked young pines, whose living needles in air and dead ones on earth offer so delicious an odor to the nostrils of the passerby, and so deadly a breath to those seedlings that would compete with them for the worthless waste they grow on.

All around for a long way were smooth fields, and the only wild tracks that ever crossed these fields were those of a thoroughly bad and unscrupulous fox that lived only too near.

The chief indwellers of the swamp were Molly and Rag. Their nearest neighbors were far away, and their nearest kin was dead. This was their home, and here they lived together, and here Rag received the training that gave him his success in life.

Molly was a good little mother and gave him a careful bringing-up. The first thing he learned was to lie low and make no noise. His adventure with the snake taught him the wisdom of this. Rag never forgot that lesson; afterward he did as instructed and it made the other things come more easily.

The second lesson he learned was to "freeze." It grows out of the first lesson, and Rag was taught it as soon as he could run.

"Freezing" is simply doing nothing, turning into a statue. As soon as he finds a foe near, no matter what he is doing, a well-trained cottontail keeps just as he is and stops all movement; for the creatures of the woods are the same color as the things in the woods and catch the eye only while moving. So when enemies chance together, the one who first sees the other can keep himself unseen by "freezing" and thus have all the advantage of choosing the time for attack or escape. Only those who live in the woods know the importance of this; every wild creature and every hunter must learn it; all learn to do it well, but not one of them can beat Molly Cottontail in the doing. Rag's mother taught him this trick by example. When the white cotton cushion that she always carried to sit on went bobbing away through the woods, of course, Rag ran his hardest to keep up. But when Molly stopped and "froze," the natural wish to copy made him do the same.

But the best lesson of all that Rag learned from his mother was the secret of the brier brush. It is a very old secret now and to make it plain, you must first hear why the brier brush quarreled with the beasts.

Long ago the roses used to grow on bushes that had no thorns. But the squirrels and mice used to climb after them; the cattle used to knock them

*off with their horns; the possum would twitch them off with his long tail;
and the deer, with his sharp hoofs, would break them down. So the brier
brush armed itself with spikes to protect its roses and declared eternal war
on all creatures that climbed trees or had horns or hoofs or long tails. This
left the brier brush at peace with none but Molly Cottontail, who could
not climb, was hornless, hoofless, and had scarcely any tail at all.*

*In truth, the cottontail had never harmed a brier rose, and having
now so many enemies, the rose took the rabbit into especial friendship.
When dangers are threatening, a poor bunny flies to the nearest brier
brush, certain that it is ready, with a million keen and poisoned daggers,
to defend him.*

So the secret that Rag learned from his mother was that the brier
brush was his best friend.

Much of the time that season was spent in learning the lay of the
land and the bramble and brier mazes. And Rag learned them so well
that he could go all around the swamp two different ways and never
leave the friendly briers at any place for more than five hops.

It had not been long since the foes of the cottontails were
disgusted to find that man had brought a new kind of bramble and
planted it in long lines throughout the country. It was so strong that
no creature could break it and so sharp that the toughest skin was
torn by it. Each year there was more of it, and each year it became a
more serious matter to the wild creatures. But Molly Cottontail had
no fear of it. She was not brought up in the briers for nothing. Dogs
and foxes, cattle and sheep, and even man himself might be torn by
those fearful spikes—but Molly understood it and lived and thrived
under it. And the farther it spread, the more safe country there was
for the cottontail. And the name of this dreaded bramble was the
barbed-wire fence.

III

Molly had no other children to look after now, so Rag had all her
care. He was unusually quick and bright as well as strong, and he had
uncommonly good chances, so he got on remarkably well.

All the season she kept him busy learning the tricks of the trail, and what to eat and drink, and what not to touch. Day by day she worked to train him; little by little she taught him, putting into his mind hundreds of ideas that her own life or early training had stored in hers, and so equipped him with the knowledge that makes life possible for their kind.

Close by her side in the clover field or the thicket he would sit and copy her when she wobbled her nose "to keep her smeller clear," and pull the bite from her mouth or taste her lips to make sure he was getting the same kind of fodder. Still copying her, he learned to comb his ears with his claws and to dress his coat and to bite the burrs out of his vest and socks. He learned, too, that nothing but clear dewdrops from the briers were fit for a rabbit to drink, as water which has once touched the earth must surely bear some taint. Thus he began the study of woodcraft, the oldest of all sciences.

As soon as Rag was big enough to go out alone, his mother taught him the signal code. Rabbits telegraph each other by thumping on the ground with their hind feet. Along the ground sound carries far; a thump that at six feet from the earth is not heard at twenty yards will, near the ground, be heard at least one hundred yards. Rabbits have very keen hearing and so might hear this same thump at two hundred yards, and that would reach from end to end of Olifant's swamp. A single *thump* means "look out" or "freeze." A slow *thump thump* means "come." A fast *thump thump* means "danger," and a very fast *thump thump thump* means "run for dear life."

At another time, when the weather was fine and the blue jays were quarreling among themselves—a sure sign that no dangerous foe was about—Rag began a new study. Molly, by flattening her ears, gave the sign to squat. Then she ran far away into the thicket and gave the thumping signal for "come." Rag set out at a run to the place, but could not find Molly. He thumped, but got no reply. Setting carefully about his search, he found her foot scent and, following this strange guide that the beasts all know so well and man does not know at all, he worked out the trail and found her where she was hidden.

Thus he got his first lesson in trailing, and thus it was that the games of hide-and-seek they played became the schooling for the serious chase of which there was so much in his later life.

Before that first season of schooling was over, he had learned all the principal tricks by which a rabbit lives and in not a few problems showed himself a veritable genius.

He was an adept at "tree," "dodge," and "squat"; he could play "log-lump," with "wind," and "baulk" with "backtrack" so well that he scarcely needed any other tricks. He had not yet tried it, but he knew just how to play "barbwire," which was a new trick of the brilliant order; he had made a special study of "sand," which burns up all scent, and he was deeply versed in "change-off," "fence," and "double," as well as "hole-up," which is a trick requiring longer notice, and yet he never forgot that "lay-low" is the beginning of all wisdom and that "brier brush," is the only trick that is always safe.

He was taught the signs by which to know all his foes and then the way to baffle them. For hawks, owls, foxes, hounds, curs, minks, weasels, cats, skunks, coons, and men each have a different plan of pursuit, and for each and all of these evils he was taught a remedy. . . . As for knowledge of the enemy's approach, he learned to depend first on himself and his mother, and then on the bluejay, for the bluejay's warnings could very well save his life.

The barbwire trick takes a deal of nerve and the best of legs. It was long before Rag ventured to play it, but as he came to his full powers it became one of his favorites. First, he led the dog on a straightaway and warmed him up a bit by nearly letting him catch him. Then keeping just one hop ahead, he led him at a long slant full tilt into a breast-high barbwire.

Rag early learned what some rabbits never learn at all—that "hole-up" is not such a fine ruse as it seems. It may be the certain safety of a wise rabbit, but sooner or later it is a sure deathtrap to a fool. A young rabbit always thinks of it first, an old rabbit never tries it till all others fail. It means escape from a man or dog, a fox or a bird of prey, but it means sudden death if the foe is a ferret, mink, skunk, or weasel.

There were but two ground holes in the swamp. One on the sunning bank, which was a dry sheltered knoll in the south end. It was open and sloping to the sun, and here on fine days the cottontails took their sunbaths. They stretched out among the fragrant pine needles and wintergreen in odd catlike positions, and turned slowly over as though roasting and wishing all sides well-done. And they blinked and panted and squirmed as if in dreadful pain; yet this was one of the keenest enjoyments they knew.

Just over the brow of the knoll was a large pine stump. Its grotesque roots wriggled out above the yellow sandbank like dragons, and under their protecting claws a sulky old woodchuck had dug a den long ago. He became more sour and ill-tempered as the weeks went by, and one day he waited to quarrel with Olifant's dog instead of going in, so that Molly Cottontail was able to take possession of the den an hour later.

This, the pine-root hole, was afterward very coolly taken by a self-sufficient young skunk who with less valor might have enjoyed greater longevity, for he imagined that even man with a gun would fly from him. Instead of keeping Molly from the den for good, therefore, his reign, like that of a certain Hebrew king, was over in seven days.

The other, the fern hole, was in a fern thicket next to the clover field. It was small and damp and useless except as a last retreat. It also was the work of a woodchuck, a well-meaning friendly neighbor, but a harebrained youngster whose skin in the form of a whiplash was now developing higher horsepower in the Olifant working team.

"Simple justice," said the old man, "for that hide was raised on stolen feed that the team would'a turned into horsepower anyway."

The cottontails were now sole owners of the holes and did not go near them when they could help it, lest anything like a path should be made that might betray these last retreats to an enemy.

There was also the hollow hickory, which, though nearly fallen, was still green, and had the great advantage of being open at both ends. This had long been the residence of one, Lotor, a solitary old coon whose ostensible calling was frog hunting, and who, like the monks of old, was supposed to abstain from all flesh food. But it was shrewdly suspected that he needed but a chance to indulge in a diet of rabbit. When at last one dark night he was killed while raiding Olifant's henhouse, Molly, so far from feeling a pang of regret, took possession of his cozy nest with a sense of unbounded relief.

IV

Bright August sunlight was flooding the swamp in the morning. Everything seemed to soak in the warm radiance. A little brown swamp sparrow was teetering on a long rush in the pond. Beneath him there were open spaces of dirty water that brought down a few scraps of the blue sky and worked it and the yellow duckweed into an exquisite mosaic, with a little wrong-side picture of the bird in the middle. On the bank behind was a great vigorous growth of golden green skunk cabbage that cast dense shadow over the brown swamp tussocks.

The eyes of the swamp sparrow were not trained to take in the color glories, but he saw what we might have missed: that two of the numberless leafy brown bumps under the broad cabbage leaves were furry living things with noses that never ceased to move up and down whatever else was still.

It was Molly and Rag. They were stretched under the skunk cabbage, not because they liked its rank smell, but because the ticks could not stand it at all and so left them in peace.

Rabbits have no set time for lessons, they are always learning; but what the lesson is depends on the present stress, and that must arrive before it is known. They went to this place for a quiet rest, but had not been there long when suddenly a warning note from the ever-watchful blue jay caused Molly's nose and ears to go up and her tail to tighten to her back. Away across the swamp was Olifant's big black-and-white dog, coming straight toward them.

Away Molly went to meet him, and she fearlessly dashed across the dog's path.

"Bow-wow-wow," he fairly yelled as he bounded after Molly, but she kept just beyond his reach and led him where the million daggers struck fast and deep, till his tender ears were scratched raw, and guided him at last plump into a hidden barbed-wire fence, where he got such a gashing that he went homeward howling with pain. After making a short double, a loop, and a baulk in case the dog should come back, Molly returned to find that Rag in his eagerness was standing bolt upright and craning his neck to see the sport.

This disobedience made her so angry that she struck him with her hind foot and knocked him over in the mud. . . .

V

There is magic in running water. Who does not know it and feel it? The railroad builder fearlessly throws his bank across the wide bog or lake, or the sea itself, but the tiniest rill of running water he treats with great respect, studies its wish and its way, and gives it all it seems to ask. The thirst-parched traveler in the poisonous alkali deserts holds back in deadly fear from the sedgy ponds till he finds one down whose center is a thin, clear line and a faint flow, the sign of running, living water, and joyfully he drinks.

There is magic in running water. . . . The wildwood creature, with its deadly foe following tirelessly on the trail scent, realizes its nearing doom and feels an awful spell. Its strength is spent, its every trick is tried in vain till it comes to the water, the running, living water, and dashing in, it follows the cooling stream, and then with force renewed takes to the woods again.

There is magic in running water. The hounds come to the very spot and halt and cast about in vain. Their spell is broken by the merry stream, and the wild thing lives its life.

And this was one of the great secrets that Raggylug learned from his mother—after the brier rose, the water was his friend.

One hot, muggy night in August, Molly led Rag through the woods. The cotton-white cushion she wore under her tail twinkled ahead and was his guiding lantern, though it went out as soon as she stopped and sat on it. After a few runs and stops to listen, they came to the edge of the pond. The hylas in the trees above them were singing *"sleep, sleep"* and away out on a sunken log in the deep water, up to his chin in the cooling bath, a bloated bullfrog was singing the praises of a *"jug o' rum."*

With a "flop," Molly went into the pond and struck out for the sunken log in the middle. Rag flinched, but plunged in, gasping and wobbling his nose very fast, but still copying his mother. The same movements as on land sent him through the water, and thus he found he could swim. On he went till he reached the sunken log and scrambled up by his dripping mother on the high dry end, with a rushy screen around them, and the water that tells no tales. After this in warm black nights when that old fox from Springfield came prowling through the swamp, Rag would note the place of the bullfrog's voice, for in case of direst need it might be a guide to safety. And thenceforth the words of the song that the bullfrog sang were, *"Come, come, in danger, come."*

This was the latest study that Rag took up with his mother—it was really a postgraduate course, for many little rabbits never learn it at all.

VI

No wild animal dies of old age. Its life has soon or late a tragic end. It is only a question of how long it can hold out against its foes. But Rag's life was proof that once a rabbit passes out of his youth he is likely to outlive his prime and be killed only in the last third of life, the downhill third we call old age.

The cottontails had enemies on every side. Their daily life was a series of escapes. For dogs, foxes, cats, skunks, coons, weasels, minks, snakes, hawks, owls, and men, and even insects were all plotting to kill them. They had hundreds of adventures, and at least once a day they had to fly for their lives and save themselves by their legs and wits.

More than once that hateful fox from Springfield drove them to take refuge under the wreck of a barbed-wire hog pen by the spring. But once there they could look calmly at him while he spiked his legs in vain attempts to reach them.

Once or twice Rag, when hunted, had played off the hound against a skunk that seemed likely to be quite as dangerous as the dog.

Once he was caught alive by a hunter who had a hound and a ferret to help him. But Rag had the luck to escape the next day, with a yet deeper distrust of ground holes. He was several times run into the water by the cat and many times was chased by hawks and owls, but for each kind of danger there was a safeguard. His mother taught him the principal dodges, and he improved on them and made many new ones as he grew older. And the older and wiser he grew, the less he trusted to his legs and the more to his wits for safety.

Ranger was the name of a young hound in the neighborhood. To train him his master used to put him on the trail of one of the cotton-tails. It was nearly always Rag that they ran, for the young buck enjoyed the runs as much as they did, the spice of danger in them being just enough for zest. . . .

On he would come, and Ranger would take the trail and follow till Rag got tired of it. Then he either sent a thumping telegram for help, which brought Molly to take charge of the dog, or he got rid of the dog by some clever trick. A description of one of these shows how well Rag had learned the arts of the woods.

He knew that his scent lay best near the ground, and was strongest when he was warm. So if he could get off the ground and be left in peace for half an hour to cool off and for the trail to stale, he knew he would be safe. When, therefore, he tired of the chase, he made for the creekside brier patch, where he "wound"—that is, zigzagged—till he left a course so crooked that the dog was sure to be greatly delayed in working it out. . . .

Ranger lost much time in the bramble maze, and the scent was very poor when he got it straightened out. Here he began to circle to pick it up. Wider and wider grew the circles, until at last he passed right under the log Rag was on. But a cold scent, on a cold day, does not go downward much. Rag never budged nor winked, and the hound passed.

Again the dog came round. This time he crossed the low part of the log and stopped to smell it. Yes, clearly it was "rabbity," but it was a stale scent now; still he mounted the log.

It was a trying moment for Rag, as the great hound came sniff-sniffing along the log. But his nerve did not forsake him; the wind was right; he had his mind made up to bolt as soon as Ranger came halfway up. But he didn't come. A yellow cur would have seen the rabbit sitting there, but the hound did not, and the scent seemed stale, so he leaped off the log, and Rag had won.

VII

Rag had never seen any other rabbit than his mother. Indeed he had scarcely thought about there being any other. He was more and more away from her now, and yet he never felt lonely, for rabbits do not hanker for company. But one day in December, while he was among the red dogwood brush, cutting a new path to the great creekside thicket, he saw all at once against the sky over the sunning bank the head and ears of a strange rabbit. The newcomer had the air of a well-pleased discoverer and soon came hopping Rag's way along one of *his* paths into *his* swamp. A new feeling rushed over him, that boiling mixture of anger and hatred called jealousy.

The stranger stopped at one of Rag's rubbing trees—that is, a tree against which he used to stand on his heels and rub his chin as far up as he could reach. He thought he did this simply because he liked it, but all buck rabbits do so, and several ends are served. It makes the tree "rabbity," so that other rabbits know that this swamp already belongs to a rabbit family and is not open for settlement. It also lets the next one know by the scent if the last caller was an acquaintance, and the height from the ground of the rubbing places shows how tall the rabbit is.

Now to his disgust Rag noticed that the newcomer was a head taller than himself and a big stout buck at that. This was a wholly new experience and filled Rag with a wholly new feeling. The spirit of murder entered his heart; he chewed very hard with nothing in his mouth, and hopping forward onto a smooth piece of hard ground he struck slowly.

"*Thump–thump–thump,*" which is a rabbit telegram for, "Get out of my swamp or fight."

The newcomer made a big V with his ears, sat upright for a few seconds, then, dropping on his forefeet, sent along the ground a louder, stronger, "*Thump–thump–thump.*"

And so war was declared.

They came together by short runs sidewise, each one trying to get the wind of the other and watching for a chance advantage. The stranger was a big, heavy buck with plenty of muscle, but one or two trifles such as treading on a turnover and failing to close when Rag was on low ground showed that he had not much cunning and counted on winning his battles by his weight. On he came at last, and Rag met him like a little fury. As they came together, they leaped up and struck out with their hind feet. *Thud, thud* they came, and down went poor little Rag. In a moment the stranger was on him with his teeth, and Rag was bitten and lost several tufts of hair before he could get up. But he was swift of foot and got out of reach. Again he charged, and again he was knocked down and bitten severely. He was no match for his foe, and it soon became a question of saving his own life.

Hurt as he was, he sprang away with the stranger in full chase and bound to kill him as well as to oust him from the swamp where he was born. Rag's legs were good and so was his wind. The stranger was big and so heavy that he soon gave up the chase, and it was well for poor Rag that he did, for he was getting stiff from his wounds as well as tired. From that day on began a reign of terror for Rag. His training had been against owls, dogs, weasels, men, and so on, but what to do when chased by another rabbit, he did not know. All he knew was to lie low till he was found then run. . . . There was no other swamp he could go to, and whenever he took a nap now he had to be ready at any moment to dash for his life. A dozen times a day the big stranger came creeping up to where he slept, but each time the watchful Rag awoke in time to escape. To escape, yet not to escape. He saved his life indeed, but, oh, what a miserable life it had become! How maddening to be thus helpless, to see all his favorite feeding grounds, the cozy nooks, and the pathways he had made with so much labor, forced from him by this hateful brute. Unhappy Rag realized that to the victor belongs the spoils, and he hated him more than ever he did fox or ferret.

How was it to end? He was wearing out with running and watching and bad food. The stranger was ready to go to all lengths to destroy poor Rag and at last stooped to the worst crime known among rabbits. However much they may hate each other, all good rabbits forget their feuds when their common enemy appears. Yet one day when a great goshawk came swooping over the swamp, the stranger, keeping well under cover himself, tried again and again to drive Rag into the open.

Once or twice the hawk nearly had him, but still the briers saved him, and it was only when the big buck himself came near being caught that he gave it up. And again Rag escaped, but was no better off. He made up his mind to leave, with his mother, if possible, the next night and go into the world in quest of some new home when he heard old Thunder, the hound, sniffing and searching about the outskirts of the swamp; and he resolved on playing a desperate game. He deliberately crossed the hound's view, and the chase that then began was fast and furious. Thrice around the swamp they went till Rag had made sure that his mother was hidden safely and that his hated foe was in his usual nest. Then right into that nest and plump over him he jumped, giving him a rap with one hind foot as he passed over his head.

Up jumped the strange rabbit only to find himself between Rag and the dog and heir to all the peril of the chase.

On came the hound baying hotly on the straightaway scent. The buck's weight and size were great advantages in a rabbit fight, but now they were fatal. He did not know many tricks. Just the simple ones like "double," "wind," and "hole-up," that every baby bunny knows. But the chase was too close for doubling and winding, and he didn't know where the holes were.

It was a straight race. The brier rose, kind to all rabbits alike, did its best, but it was no use. The baying of the hound was fast and steady. The crashing of the brush and the yelping of the hound each time the briers tore his tender ears were borne to the two rabbits where they crouched in hiding. But suddenly these sounds stopped, there was a scuffle, and then no sound at all.

Rag knew what it meant, and it sent a shiver through him, but he soon forgot that when all was over and rejoiced to be once more the master of the dear old swamp.

VIII

Old Olifant had doubtless a right to burn all those brush piles in the east and south of the swamp and to clear up the wreck of the old barbed-wire hog pen just below the spring. But it was nonetheless hard on Rag and his mother. The first were their various residences and outposts, and the second their grand fastness and safe retreat.

They had so long held the swamp and felt it to be their very own in every part and suburb—including Olifant's grounds and build-ings—that they would have resented the appearance of another rabbit even about the adjoining barnyard

Their claim, that of long, successful occupancy, was exactly the same as that by which most nations hold their land, and it would be hard to find a better right.

During the time of the January thaw Olifant had cut the rest of the large wood about the pond and curtailed the cottontails' domain on all sides. But they still clung to the dwindling swamp, for it was their home, and they were loath to move to foreign parts. Their life of daily perils went on, but they were still fleet of foot, long of wind, and bright of wit. Of late they had been somewhat troubled by a mink that had wandered upstream to their quiet nook. A little judicious guidance had transferred the uncomfortable visitor to Olifant's henhouse. But they were not yet quite sure that he had been properly looked after. So for the present they gave up using the ground holes, which were, of course, dangerous blind alleys, and stuck closer than ever to the briers and the brush piles that were left.

That first snow was quite gone, and the weather was bright and warm until now. Molly, feeling a touch of rheumatism, was somewhere in the lower thicket seeking a teaberry tonic. Rag was sitting in the weak sunlight on a bank in the east side. The smoke from the familiar gable chimney of Olifant's house came fitfully drifting, a pale blue haze through the underbrush and showing as a dull brown against the brightness of the sky. The sun-gilt gable was cut off midway by the banks of brier brush that, purple in shadow, shone like rods of blazing crimson and gold in the light. Beyond the house, the barn with its gable and roof, new gilt as the house, stood up like a Noah's ark.

The sounds that came from it, and yet more, the delicious smell that mingled with the smoke, told Rag that the animals were being fed cabbage in the yard. Rag's mouth watered at the idea of the feast. He blinked and blinked as he snuffed its odorous promises, for he loved cabbage dearly. But then he had been to the barnyard the night before after a few paltry clover tops, and no wise rabbit would go two nights running to the same place.

Therefore he did the wise thing. He moved across where he could not smell the cabbage and made his supper of a bundle of hay that had been blown from the stack. Later, when about to settle for the night, he was joined by Molly, who had taken her teaberry and then eaten her frugal meal of sweet birch near the sunning bank.

Meanwhile the sun had gone about his business elsewhere, taking all his gold and glory with him. Off in the east a big black shutter came pushing up, rising higher and higher; it spread over the whole sky, shut out all light and left the world a very gloomy place indeed. Then another mischief-maker, the wind, taking advantage of the sun's absence, came on the scene and set about brewing trouble. The weather turned colder and colder; it seemed worse than when the ground had been covered with snow. . . .

The hollow hickory was gone—in fact at this very moment its trunk, lying in the wood yard, was harboring the mink they feared. So the cottontails hopped to the south side of the pond and, choosing a brush pile, they crept under and snuggled down for the night, facing the wind but with their noses in different directions so as to go out different ways in case of alarm. The wind blew harder and colder as the hours went by, and about midnight a fine, icy snow came

ticking down on the dead leaves and hissing through the brush heap. It might seem a poor night for hunting, but that old fox from Springfield was out. He came pointing up the wind in the shelter of the swamp and chanced in the lee of the brush pile, where he scented the sleeping cottontails. He halted for a moment, then came stealthily sneaking up toward the brush under which his nose told him the rabbits were crouching. The noise of the wind and the sleet enabled him to come quite close before Molly heard the faint crunch of a dry leaf under his paw. She touched Rag's whiskers, and both were fully awake just as the fox sprang on them; but they always slept with their legs ready for a jump. Molly darted out into the blinding storm. The fox missed his spring, but followed like a racer, while Rag dashed off to one side.

There was only one road for Molly; that was straight up the wind, and bounding for her life she gained a little over the unfrozen mud that would not carry the fox, till she reached the margin of the pond. No chance to turn now, on she must go.

Splash! Splash! Through the weeds she went then plunged into the deep water.

And plunge went the fox close behind. But it was too much for Reynard on such a night. He turned back, and Molly, seeing only one course, struggled through the reeds into the deep water and struck out for the other shore. But there was a strong headwind. The little waves, icy cold, broke over her head as she swam, and the water was full of snow that blocked her way like soft ice or floating mud. The dark line of the other shore seemed far, far away, with perhaps the fox waiting for her there.

But she laid her ears flat to be out of the gale and bravely put forth all her strength with wind and tide against her. After a long, weary swim in the cold water, she had nearly reached the farther reeds when a great mass of floating snow barred her road; then the wind on the bank made strange, foxlike sounds that robbed her of all force, and she drifted far backward before she could get free from the floating bar.

Again she struck out, but slowly—oh, so slowly now. And when at last she reached the lee of the tall reeds, her limbs were numbed, her strength spent, her brave little heart was sinking, and she cared no more whether the fox was there or not. Through the reeds she did indeed pass, but once in the weeds her course wavered and slowed, her feeble strokes no longer sent her landward, the ice forming around her stopped her altogether. In a little while the cold, weak limbs ceased to move, the furry nose tip of the little mother cottontail wobbled no more, and the soft brown eyes were closed in death.

* * * * *

But there was no fox waiting to tear her with ravenous jaws. Rag had escaped the first onset of the foe, and as soon as he regained his wits he went running back to change off and so help his mother. He met the old fox going round the pond to meet Molly and led him far and away, then dismissed him with a barbed-wire gash on his head and came to the bank and sought about and trailed and thumped. But all his searching was in vain; he could not find his little mother. He never saw her again, and he never knew whither she went, for she slept her never-waking sleep in the ice arms of her friend the water that tells no tales.

Poor little Molly Cottontail! She was a true heroine, yet only one of unnumbered millions that, without a thought of heroism, have lived and done their best in their little world—and died. She fought a good fight in the battle of life. She was good stuff, the stuff that never dies. For flesh of her flesh and brain of her brain was Rag. She lives in him and through him transmits a finer fiber to her face.

And Rag still lives in the swamp. Old Olifant died that winter, and the unthrifty sons ceased to clear the swamp or mend the wire fences. Within a single year it was a wilder place than ever; fresh trees and brambles grew, and falling wires made many cottontail castles and last retreats that dogs and foxes dared not storm. And there to this day lives Rag. He is a big strong buck now and fears no rivals. He has a large family of his own and a pretty brown wife that he got I know not where. There, no doubt, he and his children's children will flourish for many years to come, and there you may see them any sunny evening if you have learned their signal code and, choosing a good spot on the ground, know just how and when to thump it.

* * * * *

"Raggylug," by Ernest Thompson Seton. Included in Seton's anthology, Wild Animals I Have Known *(New York: Doubleday, 1898). Ernest Thompson Seton (1860–1946) was born in South Shields, England, and moved to Canada in 1866. He is considered to be the founder of animal fiction writing as well as a prolific writer of nature stories. He was instrumental in founding the Boy Scouts of America and the organization Woodcraft Indians.* Wild Animals I Have Known *and* Animal House *are two of his bestsellers.*

PLUTO, THE TALKING CROW

Mary W. Caswell

*It is said that crows are incapable of human speech, unless their
tongues are split—but since no one told Pluto that, he spoke anyhow.
His talent was not without its consequences—eventually, he was
barred from church, and his bride left him!*

* * * * *

He was one of four baby crows that an adventurous boy had
taken from a nest in a tall tree and carried home for pets. In that

capacity, they all were amusing and
playful and thrived abundantly; but
Pluto was the only one to develop any
conversational ability, and in him, it was
unassisted by surgical treatment despite
the widely accepted theory that a crow is
unable to use human language unless its
tongue is split. His remained intact, but
he articulated the words that he used
more distinctly than any crow or parrot
that I ever heard speak. I never heard

him try to pronounce a word containing the letter *s*. Whether this was accidental, or because the sibilant was beyond his powers, I could not discover.

No effort had been made to teach him to speak up to the occasion when he first exhibited his talent. It was on a hot summer afternoon, and half a dozen boys had started for the swimming hole. Pluto, perched on his young master's shoulder, seemed to listen with interest as the boy urged a lagging urchin to mend his pace. "Come along, Bub!" he shouted impatiently; and was much surprised to hear croaked, directly into his ear, *"Come along, Bub!"* in very human accents! The other boys at once crowded around the pair, warmly urging Pluto to "say it again," though only half believing that the bird had really spoken, especially as he remained as mute as a Delphic oracle for the rest of the day.

The next morning, however, his master's little sister ran in from her play, calling, "Ma, I want a cup of milk!" Pluto, hopping behind her, repeated her demand with every inflection used by the child. From that time the floodgates of speech were opened, and he talked continually. It could not be said that he was teachable. Attempts to persuade him to repeat desired words or sentences he treated with lofty indifference, and proceeded to converse according to his own ideas.

His three brothers—or sisters—soon heeded the call of the wild and disappeared into the woods, but Pluto preferred human society; and remained with the family of his captor until it moved to another state. He then attached himself to a playmate of his former master, who had often come to the house, and took up his residence in the home of his new master in the neighboring village of St. Francis. But he soon forsook these living arrangements for the home of a little girl whose red hair seemed to be the object of his special admiration. He would stand on the back of her chair, his head cocked adoringly to one side, and his eyes fixed in rapture on the brilliant sheen of her locks, occasionally smoothing them gently with his beak. This rather embarrassed Rosa, particularly when he would succeed in getting into the schoolroom, as he sometimes did, and there manifest his devotion to her crowning glory. But as she was a pretty child and a great favorite, it was not as annoying as it might have been. "Only think," said her amused teacher, "if he had singled out some redheaded girl with a freckled face and snub nose! The poor child would have been laughed out of school, but with Rosa it doesn't matter."

Pluto's regard for his little mistress did not prevent his enjoying a joke at her expense, however, and there was one trick he never wearied of playing upon her. When she took her dolls' clothing to the side porch to perform the solemn rite of their family washing (in a washbasin), he would wait patiently, out of sight, until she was called away. Then he would seize one side of the basin in his strong beak and tip it to pour out the water, afterward perching complacently nearby and greeting her on her return with a prolonged *"Ha, ha, ha, ha!"*

It was a much discussed question in the village as to how much Pluto understood of what he said, but if he did not comprehend the full force of his remarks, he certainly had extraordinary luck in applying them appropriately on a great many occasions. Probably his favorite sentences were those easy to pronounce; at all events, his words were always timely, if not wholly courteous. He never spoke the name of anyone, calling everything living *"Bub,"* from white-haired Grandpa Randall to his adored little Rosa.

One morning Pluto was perched on the railing of the bridge over the Windego River, placidly watching the river-drivers pilot the logs to the sluiceway of the dam. They had been warned that he was a pet and told of his accomplishment; but they were frankly skeptical, especially as he sat speechless and almost motionless for an hour or so.

"Talk, nothin'!" growled one of them. "I bet it ain't even alive. Them kids have just stuck a stuffed crow up there. They was stringin' us along, to keep us a-listenin' for the old feather-duster. I'm going to knock it into the river." He picked up a loose piece of bark to throw, but at that moment Pluto twisted his head slightly toward him and philosophically observed, *"You look like a bloomin' fool!"*

The man dropped the bark in openmouthed surprise, but joined good-naturedly in the shouts of laughter at his expense. Work was instantly suspended, and everyone crowded toward the bridge to investigate the phenomenon more closely. One young fellow, in his eagerness to arrive within conversation range, stepped on a rolling log and was tipped into the water with a great splash. The crow, seeming to consider this mishap as a successful practical joke played by himself, seesawed gleefully back and forth, calling out in the most jovial tones, *"Hello, Bub, where you goin'?"*

This was enough to establish his reputation once and for all with the river-drivers, as it was entirely in line with their own direct and primitive ideas of humor. When, after some minutes, during which they showed no intention of returing to work, but occupied their time razzing the crow, Pluto suddenly admonished them, *"Hurry up, you'll be late for dinner!"* They accepted his advice as the acme of refined sarcasm, and, fluently encouraged by the foreman of the drive, again devoted themselves to their task of shepherding reluctant logs in the way they should go.

Although he assumed a blasé and world-weary demeanor, Pluto was visibly puffed up by their applause, and allowed himself to be persuaded to go not only to the dinner he had mentioned, but to their other meals for the two or three days they were at work at St. Francis. When the dinner bell rang, he would hop up to the shoulder of some favored youth and ride gravely to the table, where he was fed to repletion by his admirers.

On the river, he soon recognized the superior facilities offered by the shoulder of the river boss, that position affording him more variety of scenery, as this official patrolled the river from the dam up to the sorting gap, and also, it is painful to add, giving him an opportunity to embellish his vocabulary with some flowers of speech hitherto unknown to him.

However, with the passing of the log drive, whereat he mourned sincerely, spending hours on the bridge rail waiting for his fascinating friends to return, the more lurid expressions of his newly acquired vocabulary gradually dropped from his memory. This was fortunate, for I fear he would hardly have survived a repetition of an incident that occurred shortly after the drivers' departure, when he strayed into the weekly prayer meeting and enriched the proceedings with some words in season that were undoubtedly scriptural, but so unbecomingly arranged and applied that the meeting broke up in disorder. Pluto's neck would assuredly have been wrung but for the tears and entreaties of Rosa, who promised to see that he was safely shut up on every future occasion of divine worship. At the time of his interruption a good deacon had been in the midst of a rather pro-longed prayer, and Pluto, unhappily, had addressed him in the language used by his beloved river boss when exhorting some dilatory worker to greater haste and efficiency!

I had often been told of this remarkable bird, and as I much wished to see and hear him, I started with a friend one afternoon to call on Rosa's mother. As it was one of the first warm days of spring and the snow had been deep, we encountered many pools of water, but skirted them successfully till we came to a veritable pond before the gate we wished to enter. Here there was no possible way of reaching the walk except by edging along a rail of the old-fashioned fence, clinging tightly with our hands to the top of it. It was not a graceful method of approach, as Pluto seemed clearly to realize, for as we came nearer the porch where he sat, he threw back his head, opened his beak widely, and rocking back and forth in evident delight, shouted out as hearty a *"Ha, ha, ha, ha, ha!"* as I ever wish to hear at my expense.

Rosa called him into the house, but either he was sulky, or so scorned our undignified approach as to consider us beneath notice, for not a word would he utter till Mrs. Morris said, "Rosa, you'll have to brush him." We were puzzled until she explained, "There's nothing he loves so much as having Rosa take a hair brush and smooth his feathers, and she has made him understand that, if she does, he must talk."

So Rosa brought the brush, and Pluto honorably fulfilled his share of the unwritten agreement. It was with no especially remarkable salutation that he greeted my friend, *"Hello! How are you today?"* or something as commonplace, but when he turned to me and said, with a malign chuckle, *"Dam went out again Monday,"* it did seem that he was more or less human, for his statement not only was historically accurate, but it was my unfortunate family that owned this malfunctioning source of water power. The crow, sitting on Rosa's lap as she energetically brushed his feathers from head to tail, certainly appeared to be astonishingly knowledgeable of current happenings!

Pluto's gift for human speech made him the object of attention by many in the village, yet it also led to the wreck of the dreams of domestic happiness which he entertained the next spring. He had found a mate and induced her to forsake the forest solitudes, beloved of crows, to join him in building a nest in the tallest tree in the little village park. It was finished without mishap, and she had been sitting on the eggs for some days, most devotedly fed by Pluto, when one morning the contemplative landlord of the inn, looking across the park from his favorite resting place on the porch, saw the proud husband fly up to the nest as usual with a toothsome morsel for his dusky bride. She had just accepted it when Pluto committed his irretrievable error, or, as the landlord said, ". . . made the worst mistake of his life."

It is to be supposed that Pluto had wooed his spouse exclusively in the crow vernacular, and that she had been entirely unaware of his linguistic accomplishments—judging by her attitude when she discovered them. At any rate, the sequence of events was as follows: Having given her the food he had brought, he solicitously inquired, using one of his favorite sentences, *"Hello, Bub, where you goin'?"*

He was soon to learn! Dropping her breakfast with precipitous haste, she emitted one terrified squawk, rose from the nest with wildly flapping wings, and fled distractedly toward her native woods, followed in equal haste and confusion by Pluto, who with frantic expostulations, pleaded with her to return.

He pleaded in vain. Late in the afternoon he came back to town, hardly recognizable. His feathers were rumpled and awry; some were missing from his tail, and altogether he was a most forlorn spectacle. Friends addressed him consolingly, but he utterly ignored them. Straight to his once-happy home he proceeded, dashed madly at the nest, tore it to pieces with viciously wielded claws and beak, and hurled the eggs to the ground. Then, without a backward glance, he flew to Rosa's house, tapped on the window as usual, and when admitted, sought refuge from his passion of grief and humiliation in the ever-welcoming lap and open arms of his staunch little protectress. There he crouched, uttering queer little moans, while Rosa hugged him to her heart, and cried and sobbed over him.

Poor Pluto! He was not the first to find that education above the level of one's kith and kin is not always an unmixed benefit. However, such is the blessed power of recuperation in all of us that he gradually became somewhat soothed and comforted by his friend's caresses, and his self-respect, which had been nearly destroyed, began to revive.

During his courtship and honeymoon he had seen very little of his human admirers, and it now seemed to occur to him that their society had some advantages over that of his unappreciative family, for he presently hopped from Rosa's knee, and after some rummaging in the nook devoted to the hair brush reserved for his use, returned dragging that implement by the handle. There was no denying that he needed its services as never before, and its vigorous use soon restored to him some outward respectability, and seemingly, a measure of inward equanimity, for he took up his life as if his romance had not been. Its only visible trace was the aversion he afterward showed to all feathered creatures and his devotion to his human friends.

* * * * *

"Pluto, the Talking Crow," by Mary W. Caswell. Published May 1918 in St. Nicholas. *Mary Caswell wrote during the first quarter of the twentieth century.*

OLD MOM

Courtney Ryley Cooper

Elephants are ruled by queens rather than kings. Courtney Cooper, herself a circus performer, remembers one unforgettable grande dame dubbed "Old Mom." In the incidents that follow, you will enter into a world you never dreamed even existed!

* * * * *

It is simple to learn elephant language. When an elephant desires to make an imperative demand, it does so by a sharp blast which is used for that purpose, and that alone. When it begs or coaxes, the trumpet call is soft and pleading, almost a whine. When one elephant is frightened and another isn't, the calm member soothes his companion by a soft announcement which carries a low and expressive note. To say nothing of the love lullaby— and, an elephant in love is as thorough about the matter as a sixteen-year-old boy—the fear signal, the danger signal,

the warning chirrup which inevitably gives the announcement of an impending stampede, the wailing cry of pain or distress by which a "bull" tells when he is ill, and lastly, the sound of gratitude or contentment. When a pachyderm thumps on the ground with his trunk to attract your attention, then places the end of his trunk in his ear using that ear as a sort of diaphragm, and blows with the softness of a reed instrument in the hands of a practiced musician, you can mark it down for certain that there's one elephant in the world that is pleased almost beyond speech!

So, perhaps it's because they understand the elephantine language that circus men like elephants. Perhaps it isn't. For the one real reason is the fact that the elephant can be the most foolish, yet at the same time, remain fundamentally the most sagacious beast of the whole animal kingdom! This goes for everything—from government on down. In elephantdom there are even elections, to say nothing of a rare case now and then of a complete change of administration.

The elephant is a strong believer in government, of the feminine sort. There aren't any male party leaders. It's the female every time that forms the head of an elephant herd and that handles the reins of administration. But one queen can be better than another, and the subjects are quick to recognize the fact!

In 1903, a Western circus, which at that time possessed an elephant herd of six members ruled by a comparatively young and inexperienced queen, decided that it needed more pachyderms. It therefore sent to Germany for two additions to the herd, with the result that a month or so later there arrived in America a determined female named Old Mom, accompanied by her equally feminine sidekick, Frieda.

Mom and Frieda had been boss and assistant boss of a herd in Germany. A wise old leader was Mom. Sixty years of age, slightly puffy under the eyes—elephants have a strange way of showing their years in much the same manner as a human—with a few teeth missing, but with a bump of sagacity and determination, which had made her outstanding even among a group of thirty elephants in Germany, Old Mom was a sort of Queen Victoria among pachyderms. A strong friendship between the owners of the animal farm in Germany and the owners of the circus had been responsible for her shipment—friendship which the circus owner looked upon a bit dubiously as he read the letter which announced her coming.

"Fine bunch Hagenbeck's handed me!" he muttered dolefully. "He's sent over an elephant that's used to running things in the herd. I've already got a leader. What'll happen when they get together? Fight their heads off, I guess."

Nor were the handlers quite sure themselves what the outcome would be; it was about the same proposition as a general manager being hired for a factory where the only executive position was already filled. With some misgivings, they led Mom and her friend, Frieda, into the menagerie tent and put them with the herd. Nothing happened. A few days went by, in which Bumps, the regular leader, continued at her job as the mainspring of the herd, Mom and her chum, Frieda, merely tagging along and doing what the rest did. Then something happened!

There wasn't a revolution; in fact, it just seemed to happen. In the herd was a young elephant that was being trained and that didn't like the procedure. On the third day after Mom's arrival, the elephant keeper placed his hook gently behind the student's ear to lead him forth to his lessons. The elephant protested, squealing as though in pain, as though the keeper were using cruelty and really plunging the hook deep in his flesh. Old Mom watched the proceeding with interest.

More, when that scholar came back to his place in line, still squealing the distress signal, Old Mom walked over to him, eyed him carefully, reached forth her trunk and very tenderly examined the skin behind the ear, as though searching for some evidence of a wound. She didn't find it; the elephant had lied about that bullhook. Immediately Old Mom gave her verdict, by tightly coiling her trunk, then sending it forth with the force of a pile driver, striking the malingerer squarely in the forehead and flooring him. After which she calmly walked back to her stake.

Immediately the picket line became a thing of low-voiced chirrups, of excited trumpeting, and of general chatter so complicated that even the animal men didn't know what it was all about. But they found out the next morning.

It was dawn, and a long haul from the circus train to the lot. The twenty-four-hour man, standing in the middle of the road, flagged down the cookhouse wagon and shouted a message. "Let the elephants go first. Two or three bridges that don't look any too safe. Better wait till the elephants have tested 'em."

Whereupon the announcement traveled on down the line to the elephant superintendent, and a moment later he passed on the run, his gigantic charges trundling after. They reached the first bridge.

"Bumps!" he shouted. But Bumps hung back. Instead, in her place, as calmly as though she had occupied the position all her life, Old Mom walked forward, followed by Frieda, placed one foot on the bridge, hefted her weight onto it, pronounced it safe, and crossed, her handmaiden close beside her, with Bumps taking third place in line. It had been accomplished overnight. The herd had found the kind of a leader it wanted—and elected her. Old Mom has been in command ever since!

Nor was ever a political boss more autocratic. Like many another leader of elephant herds, Old Mom has her system, which runs from rewards to punishments, from beating up the male members or agitators to soothing the feelings of some squealing "punk," fresh from its fright of the first lesson in elephant training. Never does Old Mom neglect to check up on the effects of the first few days at school. With the sensitive "finger" of her trunk working with the exactness of a measuring tape, she covers, inch by inch, the spots where the ropes have been tied to trip the animal in the process of teaching it to lie down, examines the spots behind the ears and along the trunk where the elephant men are wont to catch the beast with their elephant hooks, looking everywhere for evidence of rope burns or cruelty. If she finds them, there is bellowing and hatred for an inefficient animal trainer, often leading to investigation by the animal superintendent and the discharge of the offending trainer. If she doesn't, which is usually the case, she merely cajoles the beast with slow-sounding, reedlike noises, gradually calming it. And if the animal persists in its foolish fears, she whacks it across the face with her trunk and walks away in disgust. The queer thing is that she is able to discern between real and bogus fright; she seems to know that her charges are naturally lazy and that they'll get out of work if they can! More than once Old Mom has been known to halt in her labors on the show lot that she might eye carefully the elephant which is working with her—or pretending to work. The best little trick that an elephant knows is to place its head within about an eighth of an inch of a wagon and pretend to push, while really not exerting an atom of effort. It often fools the elephant men. But it doesn't fool Old Mom. One whirling blow of that trunk, and Mom herself does the resting.

But her trunk isn't Mom's only weapon. There are nineteen elephants in her herd now, and some of them are bigger than she. A battle of trunks might result in a disheveled queen. So Mom has other and more judicious methods. One of these is to seize the ear of an offender with a quick thrust of her trunk, cramp it hard, then twist. It never has failed yet to produce a bellowing, howling subject, suddenly brought to his knees and begging for mercy. Another gentle trick is to whirl suddenly, lower her head, and with all her strength, butt a criminal in the midriff.

Three years ago, a full-grown male elephant was purchased from another show where the rules of the herd leader evidently had been a trifle lax. For four or five days the new member gave evidences of resenting the stern rule of Old Mom. Then suddenly everything changed. He was the meekest member of the whole herd. All his bluster and rebellion had vanished. Also, three inches of his tail. Old Mom had made one swirling dive, caught his caudal appendage between her teeth, and clamped hard while fourteen thousand pounds of elephant flesh trumpeted and bellowed and squealed, and while the whole menagerie force struggled to break the hold. When it was all over, an operation was necessary to remove the crushed cartilage and bone. One of Old Mom's very best boys now is a bobtailed elephant!

As for punishment for herself, she recognizes but one superior: the superintendent of the herd. To him and him alone she acknowledges the right of punishment, even makes ready for it. In 1914, one of the stars of the show was William Frederick Cody (Buffalo Bill), and in his employ was a former officer of the Russian Army who, through the nonchalance of the circus, had become simply "Rattlesnake Bill."

Rattlesnake Bill teased Old Mom, and the elephant hated him so much that it became almost an obsession with her to get him. This she attempted at every opportunity, chasing him when she saw the chance, striving to sneak up on him—she could release any chain tie ever made by human hands—and once almost catching him, and, failing, taking out her vengeance on Colonel Cody's carriage which Rattlesnake Bill drove, wrecking it. Then suddenly she halted at the sight of the superintendent.

A bullhook lay on the ground. She reached for it, raised it, and extended it to her keeper, offering it to him that he might punish her. But before he could raise his arm, she had begun to "talk," chirruping in his ear, curling her trunk around his neck, cooing at him with that peculiar blandishing tone, which in its very softness, seems impossible for an elephant. Then finally, whimpering, she went to her knees. If ever an elephant talked herself out of a well-deserved whack across the trunk, it was Old Mom, with the result that she returned to her place at the stake line victorious, while an order went forth that Rattlesnake Bill, in the future, must leave the elephants alone!

In fact, it is such evidences of reasoning power and of quick thinking that make the elephant such a beloved thing to the circus man. . . .

This has its counterpart in the actions of the herd of another circus, which suddenly appeared on the streets of a Canadian town, each waving a gunnysack in very stolid and dignified fashion, as it marched along in parade. The crowds in the street didn't know what it was all about, nor did a good part of the show, for that matter. Behind it was a theft, a fight, the hint of an elephant insurrection, and a great invention. Archimedes accomplished no more when he discovered the principle of the screw!

It was fly time—and hard ground. There was little dust for the elephants to curl into their trunks and throw on their backs, thus ridding themselves of the pests. The herd was becoming fidgety when Old Mom, the leader, noticed something before her, eyed it thoughtfully, then reached forth her trunk to seize it. A gunnysack.

She waved it on the right side, and the flies departed. She tried the other side, then straight over her head. Her back was free! Old Mom shimmied with delight, then draping the gunnysack over one ear, she poked her trunk into the other, to announce a squeal of discovery and of happiness. But while she was doing this, the next elephant in line stole the sack!

Immediately there was trouble. The flies had returned, and Old Mom wanted her sack. But the thief pretended not to notice. Whereupon Old Mom whanged him on the proboscis.

He dropped the sack. But before Old Mom could retrieve it, the third elephant borrowed the fly duster, and when excited animal handlers returned with the elephant superintendent, four fights were in progress, while the sack was traveling here and there about the stake line like a football. There was a quick command, then peace. Every elephant was equipped with his own personal flyswatter, and what is more, they were retained, each being carefully carried to the cars at night when the great, shadowy herd thumped through the semidarkness for its journey to the next town.

Impossible? That an elephant should think of such things? Talk for a while with a circus man who really knows elephants, and you'll find it is only the beginning! . . .

* * * * *

If there were such things as false teeth for elephants, Mom probably would have had them. Nature fitted her with a poor dental display, and around the menagerie in which she is the herd-head the attendants are almost constantly dosing her for anything from sore gums to cavities. There came a time when Mom produced a tooth which needed pulling.

It caused a conference. The superintendent knew that he couldn't rummage around in her mouth with a pair of forceps and yank out that tooth with a block and tackle. Besides, there was no way to chain her sufficiently for a slow, pulling process. In addition, animal men, propagandists to the contrary, are as a rule softhearted.

So, the task with Mom was to get that tooth out as quickly as possible, and with a minimum of pain. The elephant superintendent drove a stake deep into the ground before Mom, sent her to her haunches, and then, as tenderly as possible, fastened one end of a piece of baling wire to the tooth and the other to the stake. Whereupon he walked away, picked up his bullhook, deliberately approached Frieda and whacked her on the trunk.

Frieda squealed as though her life were in danger, and Mom jerked to her feet, bellowed, stared in goggle-eyed fashion, then, suddenly forgetful of the animal she had sought to succor, jammed her trunk into her mouth, felt about carefully, and squealed happily. The tooth lay on the ground, where it had been yanked by the baling wire as Mom jumped to her feet! It was the old story over again of the boy and a piece of twine tied to the doorknob. Human remedies work with elephants also, even to the extent of paregoric when they get colic. . . .

* * * * *

They're a constant round of mischief, those elephants. Something's always happening. The show train was on a downgrade one morning, late, and fighting to make up time so that it might at least stand a chance of giving a performance that afternoon. Suddenly the emergency brakes clamped hard, performers scattered around the sleeping cars, animals howled, cages slipped from their fastenings and began to wobble about the flat cars as the air pressure was exerted its utmost to halt the progress of the speeding section. The conductor, nonplussed, scrambled along the flats, reaching the first one just as the train halted.

"What're you stopping for?" he shouted to the engineer.

"Ask yourself the same question!" came the retort. "You flagged me down."

"You're crazy!"

"Am I? Well, take a look for yourself; your brakeman's still at it!"

The conductor looked back along the train. Far in the rear, atop a car, a big piece of canvas was being waved wildly, frantically. Still wondering, the conductor retraced his steps.

The train had passed through a small town a short time before. On the next track had been a flat car loaded with a new automobile, which, in turn was covered by a tarpaulin. The opportunity had been too good to miss. Old Mom had reached out between the bars of the elephant car, yanked the tarpaulin off on the fly, dragging it into the car, played tug-of-war with it for a time with the rest of the elephants, distributing pieces to the remainder of the herd as the tarpaulin was torn to shreds, then, in an ecstasy of play, had looked about for a place high enough in which she might wave what was left over her head. This had been provided in a ventilator, which she had shoved open, and through which she had extended her trunk with the canvas waving to the winds. But up ahead the engineer had known nothing of the nature of elephants. He had seen only trouble, and he had clamped on those emergency brakes.

To tell the truth, clamping on the emergency brake is about the most frequent thing happening around the circus when the elephants are concerned. No one ever is able to tell what they're going to do or when they're going to do it. Their prankishness runs the whole gamut of everything that ever entered the head of a ten-year-old boy and their curiosity is worse than that of a monkey. . . .

* * * * *

It is necessary, except when a long run is to be made and a tremendous distance bridged between two towns, for a circus to "Sunday on the lot"; that is: to set up its tents, clean the circus from end to end, repaint poles, repair damage that has been done during the hard traveling of the week, rest the horses and animals, and in general make ready for another six days of constant effort and fighting against time that the show may live true to its billing and its promises of "two performances a day, rain or shine." It is a time of general overhauling and of rest, a time of relaxation—the elephants' delight, and the bull-man's misery. For it is during Sunday on the lot—just as it is with a great many small boys on Sunday—that the elephants think up most of their prankishness. When an elephant becomes mischievous, it costs money.

One Sunday night in Texas, the night watchman, making his final rounds, noticed that every elephant stood sleepily at the picket pin, and then rolled under a lion cage for a few hours' sleep of his own. Dawn came, and he awoke. All the elephants were still there; everything was quiet. But not so an hour later!

An irate brickyard keeper had appeared, with a sleepy-eyed attorney hastily summoned from bed. The elephants had ruined his place during the night! A brick kiln had been demolished, piles of bricks scattered and destroyed, the mixer overturned and broken, and the various stacks of tile shattered. The elephants had done it. There began the argument.

The elephants couldn't have done it; they hadn't been out of the menagerie! The night watchman testified to the fact; the menagerie workers told of having seen the elephants when they left at night and when they arrived at dawn, perfectly peaceable at the stake line. The argument grew warmer. The legal adjuster was summoned, and then someone suggested that they go to the brickyard.

There the evidence was irrefutable. Everywhere were the big tracks of an elephant, and the chase led back to the circus. There was no way to controvert the statements of the brickyard owner now. There were no other elephants within a thousand miles. And so the search for the culprit began, to finish as rapidly. Old Mom, the leader of the herd, had been caught red-handed.

Or rather, red-legged. The whole rear expanse of her hind legs, from her hoofs to her hips, was beautifully rouged with brick dust, where she had backed up to a pile of bricks and scratched herself! She had untied the half hitch of her chain from the picket stake, carefully carried it in her trunk, gone under the side wall, enjoyed a night out, wrecked the brickyard, then returned to the menagerie tent, and with one twisting toss—a trick, incidentally, which she took delight in teaching other elephants—had placed that half hitch back on the stake again!

Nor was Old Mom's trick unusual. It seems characteristic of elephants to desire to take a night out for themselves every so often. . . .

* * * * *

"Inconsistency—thy name is elephant!"

For, it seems, the paradox is a continual thing with the great pachyderms which form the backbone of practically every circus. There is never a time when they are not depended upon to save the show in times of late arrivals, muddy or sandy lots, or on long hauls from the unloading runs to the exhibition grounds, when the two or three tons of flesh and bone and muscle, which every elephant possesses, are thrown into play to augment the efforts of the straining draft animals and chugging tractors. Yet, by the same token, upon one man and one alone—the keeper of the herd—depends the task of keeping them the placid, humorous clowns which they really should be.

In explanation, a herd of elephants—and in some of the big circuses a herd will number as high as twenty-five members—is built upon the monarchial system, with a princess or two, a queen and a king in control. The princesses and queen are elephants; the only male ruler allowed is the superintendent of the herd, the man to whom the queen, or leader, vows allegiance. No matter what other men may do, what other men may command, if the keeper of the herd decides otherwise, then otherwise is the result. The leader obeys him above all others; the princesses obey her, and the male members tag along in a group of bulky camp followers, citizens, agitators, and revolutionists. The males make the trouble in an elephant monarchy; the females make the laws and enforce them.

As an example, Old Mom and her herd were in Canada several years ago, and one of its stands was Winnipeg. The performances were dated for Monday and, as is usual with a circus, the show had arrived in town a day ahead. The tents had been erected, the seats placed, the animals fed and exercised, the ring curbs fastened into position, the hippodrome track smoothed into readiness, the rigging for the various aerial acts set, and the circus had settled to rest.

In the menagerie, the lions and tigers nodded sleepily, with nothing to disturb them from their Sunday slothfulness. The elephant picket line was calm and peaceful, the long trunks weaving lazily at the transference of a full portion of roughage from ground to mouth. Group by group the circus people departed from the lot, townward bound, for the usual Sunday stroll and the luxury of a night in a hotel instead of the cramped berths of the sleepers. Only the watchmen were left about the various tents; only the assistants in the menagerie.

Night came, starlit and peaceful. The torches began to gleam about the circus grounds, spots of limited brilliance barely sufficient to provide protection against the pitfalls of stakes and wagon tongues and tight-pulled guy ropes. Hours passed in torpid peace. Downtown the superintendent of the elephant herd, Fred Alispaw, seated himself at the table of a late-night restaurant and glanced across toward his wife, awaiting her decision on the menu. He called a waiter. He began the giving of an order. Then suddenly the café, the street, the city were in darkness, following a green blaze of lightning and its consequent crash of thunder. A moment more and the rain was pelting, borne at the fore of a forty-mile gale. Winnipeg, all in a second, had become a storm-stricken city; its lights extinguished by a lightning bolt which had struck one of the main feed wires, its streetcar service blocked, its streets running small rivers from the rain, its every activity for the moment halted. In the café diners laughed, struck matches, and waited for the lights to come on again—all but one man, stumbling through the darkness toward the doorway, Fred Alispaw, keeper of the herd.

"Stay here until the lights come on!" he ordered hastily of his wife. "I've got to get to the lot!"

"But the cars are stopped."

"Can't help that. I'll find a taxi! I've got to get to the lot!"

Out into the sheetlike rain he went, to leap to the running board of the first passing automobile and literally commandeer it for a trip to the circus grounds several miles away. His experience with elephants and the instinctive knowledge of what the beasts might do under circumstances such as this demanded swift action, and plenty of it. More, intuition proved correct!

The storm had struck as suddenly at the circus grounds as in the city. With the first flash of lightning, the wind had swept through the menagerie tent with gale-like force, lifting the side wall and causing it to slap and bellow and snap in queer ghostly fashion. The elephant herd, peaceful and drowsing at its double row of stakes only a moment before, had heard and seen!

There was no keeper to reassure them—only assistants. To an elephant an assistant counts for little if the supreme voice is absent, and right at that moment Alispaw was miles away. In vain the menagerie men sank their bullhooks into the ears of plunging charges, then, bobbing about like so many plummets, strove in vain to hold the beasts in line. Even Old Mom, the head of the herd, had become panicky with the rest, not from fear of the storm but from the fright caused by the sight of that twisting, writhing side wall as it had shown for an instant in the glare of the lightning. To the elephants it represented some unknown bellowing monster about to attack; the unexplained thing always means trouble in an elephant herd. So the stampede had begun.

One by one, the extra stakes were dragged from the ground. One by one, the frantic animal attendants were thrown aside or knocked down by the flail-like blows of tossing trunks. The thunder now bore an obbligato of screaming, hissing cat animals, crouched in fear in their dens, of shouting men, of rending stakes, clanking chains, and squealing, trumpeting elephants. Then still another thunder, that of ton-heavy bodies plunging across the menagerie tent, the crashing of timbers as they knocked poles and cages from their path, and the stampede of the nine-elephant herd was on! A moment later the stakes, the poles, the seats and grandstand of the main tent were splintering and snapping as some sixty thousand pounds of fear-maddened elephant flesh tore madly here and there in a big enclosure, rushing wildly, then wheeling as frantically in the other direction as a lightning flash showed that writhing, flapping thing of windblown canvas surrounding them on every side. Greater and greater the frenzy became; in the milling, two of the males collided and began to fight with swift smashing rushes and lashing trunks. Louder and louder became the squealing and trumpeting—suddenly to lull. A voice had come faintly from the darkness of the menagerie tent—every torch long had been extinguished—a voice which caused Old Mom to turn and to trumpet with a new note.

"Mom! Mom! Here I am!"

Again the call sounded, and Old Mom answered, the queen obeying the command of her overlord. The fighting ceased. A new signal sounded from the throat of Old Mom. The elephants steadied. A moment later Alispaw, standing in the vestibule between the menagerie and the main tent, saw revealed in a flash of lightning a great hulking shadow coming slowly but steadily toward him, while in the rear there followed eight others, practically abreast! Old Mom had heard the voice she sought. That was enough!

But the fight had only begun. The storm now was taking on a new intensity, a new fury, and the trainer knew that he had but two allies: Mom and Frieda, her elephantine lady-in-waiting. As soon as possible, the keeper caught the two elephants by their ears and stood between them, talking to them, reassuring them, while they wrapped their trunks about him and squealed their delight, while the rest of the herd milled and trumpeted about them, each crowding its utmost to be near the thing which to them meant safety. For nearly an hour it continued, with the fate of the show in the hands of one man, literally buried in a bumping, jostling mass of thirty tons of frightened elephants—one man whom they trusted and whose presence alone could hold them against a new panic. Then slowly, with the aid of his assistants and a lone flickering torch, he began the task of working the mammals back to their picket line.

For Mom and for Frieda, it was comparatively easy. For the rest, it was a far more difficult task. Alispaw could not be in every place at once, and the moment the herd became strung out to the slightest degree there would be a concerted rush to be near the lead elephants and the keeper who guided them. In vain the assistants strove to drive them back, and at last one of the men, losing his head, struck violently at one of the beasts with an iron-tipped tent stake, only to miscalculate. The blow struck Alispaw, and he dropped unconscious; the note of fright in Old Mom's bellow brought a new spasm of fear and a resumption of the milling to the rest of the herd.

Once more they circled and crowded—all but one. That one was Old Mom, half-crouched over the prostrate trainer, whimpering and touching him with her trunk, and through her frightened curiosity, forming a bulwark against the rest of the surging herd. For a full five minutes this continued, then, dizzy and reeling, the keeper crawled to his feet and renewed his calls of assurance. The storm lessened. Slowly Old Mom wheeled into place at the picket line and submitted to her chains. Frieda came beside her; then, still trembling, still grunting and squealing and protesting, the rest followed. Daylight found the picket line again a thing of comparatively peaceful elephants, and all because of one man!

* * * * *

With it all, the life of an elephant keeper is a thing of constant gambling. He has none of the assurances with which the performers of other beasts are blessed; the lion or tiger trainer has his cages, and the knowledge that even should a vicious cat escape, a bullet or two from a heavy-caliber revolver at close range can finish him. It takes a steel-jacketed army bullet to make an elephant even realize he's being shot!

Moreover, the beasts are too big to be caged. They are too strong for anything except a perfect network of drop-forged chains. Even then, nothing short of a pile driver can set wood deep enough into the ground to hold them when they really desire to run. It's wholly a matter of a good leader of the herd, good princesses working under her, the hope that there are few agitators or revolutionists in the rest of the monarchy, and a strong trust in fate and the breaks of circumstance. For even the elephant keeper never knows what may start his difficulties. An invasion of fleas in the sandy districts of the West can do it; an elephant's hide can turn a leaden revolver bullet, but it can't stand fleas! There's trouble even in mosquitoes.

For the flea and the mosquito evidently have more judgment regarding the points of vulnerability in an elephant's hide than does a bullet. They select the soft spots behind the ears, the eyelids and tender mouth and flanks for their work, and once they arrive in numbers, trouble begins. It is not at all unusual to see elephants being dosed with flea preventives. The mosquito pest is far more rare, but at least one runaway is chargeable to this cause.

Incidentally, the instance gave another credit mark to the career of Old Mom and another example of at least one elephant with common sense. The show was making a Sunday run in Canada by which it bridged a long expanse of territory between moneymaking stands, heading far into the north of the Dominion, where few shows had exhibited and where the natives would be glad to part with a double admission price for the pleasure of seeing a bigger circus than usual. The run had been preceded by several days of moist, mosquito-breeding weather, with the result that when the show train made a feed stop at a small prairie settlement, and the elephants were unloaded for a trip of half a mile to the nearest water, the insects swarmed in such millions that they almost obliterated the lettering of the railroad cars. About the railroad tracks several hundred smudges were lighted, thus freeing that exact territory from the pests, but the elephants weren't fortunate. They were forced to travel out into the country for water, and the mosquitoes went with them.

By the time the watering process was finished every elephant was crusted with stinging, poisonous insects and squealing with discomfort. They pulled from their keepers; in vain Old Mom, obeying the commands of Alispaw, strove to hold them in line. She bellowed, she butted, then lashed with her trunk—but to no purpose. A moment more, and an inveterate agitator made the break, followed by two others, and instantly the rest of the herd rushed after them. More, Old Mom broke from the bullhooked grasp of her keeper, and with Frieda, her handmaiden, beside her, swung madly into flight also!

It seemed that at last the ability of Old Mom to command a situation was lost. Faster and faster she went, passing the slower members of the herd and at last forcing her way to the very front of the stampede, Frieda puffing along in her wake. For a full eighth of a mile she led the rush straight out into the prairie. Then the pursuers, far in the rear, noticed that she was beginning to turn in her course. Soon she had made a semicircle and was leading the plunging herd straight back in the direction of the cars.

Thundering on they went, the workmen and clustered performers parting spasmodically as they approached the runs, Old Mom still in the lead, and heading, it seemed, on a straight path for the sleeping cars and the crash which seemed inevitable. Once an elephant loses its head, it takes no cognizance of what may be before it; its mind knows a beeline only, no matter if the obstruction be a stone quarry.

Nearer, nearer! Then it suddenly became evident that Old Mom evidently was in full possession of her faculties—and a bright idea. At the tracks she swerved, and while horses and workmen scurried for safety, she led the way straight to the elephant cars and climbed in!

The runs, or running board by which the beasts usually made their entrance and exit had been removed in preparation for the switching of the cars. So the climbing operation was a literal one. With the rest of the elephants behind her, Old Mom, grunting and squealing, made the ascent, and Frieda followed.

Then in the semidarkness of the smudge-filled car she trumpeted happily, and the rest of the herd crowded in after her. A stampede of nearly a mile was over without a cent of damage.

In fact, Old Mom, with her faith and her levelheadedness, has meant salvation in many an instance. I once saw this sensible old elephant lead her herd across the cable bridge which connects Wheeling, West Virginia, with the Ohio side, with a storm in progress, the surroundings inky black, the rain pelting, the keepers almost as terrified as the brutes, with the beams of the bridge cracking from overweight, and the structure itself swinging fully eight feet from side to side! Below was a sheer drop to the Ohio River; two elephants had become panic-stricken and had broken from the bull-man in attendance, rushing frantically forward to the protection of their leader. The rest of the herd had begun to mill, with only a thirty-foot width of bridge as their arena; the keepers were befuddled and nearly blinded by the pelting rain. Yet Old Mom held true to the commands of her trainer, and with weird trumpetings, which sounded sharp above even the rush of wind and crackling of thunder, someway, somehow, reassured her herd. Then with the ever-present Frieda at her side, she began to lead the way, slow step after slow step to the opposite side.

That very slowness was the salvation of the herd; instinctively they knew that she was testing the bridge, and by some sort of animal understanding, did likewise. The rocking lessened. A half hour later, Old Mom brought her charges safe out at the other side, every elephant walking in comical, gingerly fashion for a full block after leaving the structure, for all the world like overgrown fat boys trying to negotiate an area of eggshells. . . .

* * * * *

Fortune sometimes favors even a keeper of elephants, and such was the case in the stampede of Old Mom's herd at Idaho Falls.

The day had been hot. The elephants came out of the performing ring of the matinee tired and "juggy," as the bull-man terms lassitude, to be led quite indifferently to a nearby irrigation ditch to drink. There, by straining against their elephant hooks, they indicated that a mere drink would not satisfy.

"What're we goin' t' do?" inquired an assistant as he scrambled at the end of a bullhook. "They want in an' they're goin' t' have in!"

"Hold them bulls!" came the curt reply of the keeper. "Sink that hook deeper an' hold them bulls."

"What's the matter?" It was a new voice. "They just want a swim, don't they?"

"Yeh." The keeper touched his cap to the owner of the show. "Yeh. That's what they're after."

"Then why don't you let 'em have it?"

"Afraid. Snake River's just over this hump here, and they might make for it. It's deep an' swift. Been a half a dozen horses drowned right here; nothing's ever come out of it alive."

"But," argued the little owner, "that isn't this ditch, is it? Why should they want to go over to a river they can't see when there's all this water right here?"

The keeper grinned in sickly fashion.

"You don't know elephants. They'll. . . ."

"Quit your kidding. Let 'em go. The poor things are hot."

"All right." The keeper sighed—a sigh with a goodbye in it. "You're the boss. Hey, men! Turn 'em loose!"

There was a rush, a splash of water, then shining bulky forms that flopped and scrambled out of the water at the other side of the irrigation ditch. The herd, in its entirety, had smelled broader expanses of water, and almost abreast they went for it—all but Old Mom, who trumpeted wildly, who squealed and bellowed and roared, but who for a moment remained alone. Even her faithful Frieda deserted her, running wildly with Snyder and Trilby over the edge of the hump and sliding down a declivity of solid rock into the raging waters of the Snake River rapids. Behind them the two remaining members of the herd halted, stood a moment in fear, then whimpering returned to the side of Old Mom, while the circus owner, believing he had sent a valuable elephant herd to its death, hurriedly decided to move elsewhere than within the range of the baleful eye of the keeper of the elephants.

Down in the rapids, with its falls and dangerous suck holes, the three elephants floundered a moment then splashed out in different directions. Frieda, her common sense aroused at last, swam with all her strength straight for the opposite shore, finally landing in safety just above the falls. But Trilby and Snyder, forgetting the swiftness of the current in their enjoyment of the water's coolness, drifted lazily along, until too late. A moment more, and the hundreds of excited sightseers who had gathered atop the banks saw the rolling, tossing, suddenly frantic beasts plunge over the falls and into the suck holes and whirlpools beneath, from which no living thing ever had emerged.

By this time the owner was far away and seeking even more speed. A man in an automobile hastened to overtake him and to break the news that his elephants were in the Snake River death trap. He nodded glumly and went on.

The elephants now were in a suck hole which formed the main amusement of the boys of the town who, when the lure of other games had faded, were wont to push large logs over the edge into the swirling waters and watch them churned to bits by the fierce action of the boiling waters. Trilby had vanished. Only the edge of Snyder's trunk showed at long intervals. Atop the bank the keeper of the elephants breathed another goodbye to two of his best elephants.

Then a shout. Fully three hundred feet below the suck hole Trilby, immersed for what had seemed hours, had come to the surface and was fighting valiantly toward shore. Finally she gained it, to crawl to a rocky ledge, to stagger, then to fall exhausted. Five minutes later, Snyder lay beside her, equally fatigued. And there they remained, moaning with almost human intonations, until their keeper, with Old Mom, came to their rescue.

All through the town the word spread that a living thing—two living things, in fact—had survived the death trap. The crowds gathered; it was as though conquering heroes had returned from a war. The townspeople even forgave Frieda and refused damages when it was learned that she had ambled from her landing point to a livery yard and caused a panic among the horses stabled there. That night the tents were unable to contain the crowds that thronged to see the elephants which had braved the whirlpools. And in the years to come, the simple announcement of the coming of the circus was enough to ensure the influx of thousands of dollars, as long as it contained the assurance that the death trap elephants would be a part of the performance.

But such a happy thing as this in the life of an elephant keeper is almost too good to be true. In the circus world the young man seeking adventure is never told to go West, nor to become a prospector, nor to drive in motorcar speed events, nor to aspire to the Northwest Mounties. It is merely suggested that if he's really in earnest and doesn't care what happens, it might be a good idea to learn the rudiments of being a keeper of the elephants. After that if he isn't satisfied, he's hopeless!

* * * * *

"Old Mom," by Courtney Ryley Cooper. Published in Cooper's book, Lions 'n' Tigers 'n' Everything *(Boston: Little, Brown, and Company, 1924). If anyone can provide knowledge of the author's next of kin, please send the information to Joe Wheeler (P. O. Box 1246, Conifer, CO 80433). Courtney Cooper (1886–1940), was born in Kansas City, Missouri, and wrote books having to do with the circus, show business, and the Old West.*

Shanee, Gallant Gentleman

Jean M. Thompson

Everything was going so well for the handsome raccoon until he started watching the antics of the cutest little striped animals he'd ever seen.

All good times now came to an untimely end.

* * * * *

The first faint suggestions of dawn had already appeared when Shanee, young raccoon, decided to leave the swamp. Skipping lightly over quaking bogs, silently and fleetly he made now for the shelter of the deep forest. He had feasted well that night, felt comfortable, and was thankful that the long hibernation of winter had ended. Now the ice prisons, which for many weary months had held the waterways in frozen grip, had melted, freeing the pent-in crayfish, the little sweet mussels, and freshwater clams which he so craved.

Shanee was both young and handsome, although at this season his beautiful coat of mixed silver and black was not in prime condition. Still, being the personification of neatness and something of a dandy, he would soon be otherwise. For with the frequent washings and grooming which he would give it, his pelt would begin to shine and thicken again. His delicately pointed snout somehow suggested breeding. The green, inquisitive eyes, set in velvety bands of black, lent to his gray face the deeply intelligent expression of some learned sage wearing horn-rimmed spectacles.

Over the undergrowth of darker fur ran other, longer hairs tipped with white which, waving as he ran, gleamed with silvery sheen. Dainty and handlike were his swift feet, leaving behind a track like the handprint of a child. These feet Shanee used with monkeylike dexterity in the preparation and cleansing of all food.

Of five raccoons born in the same litter, Shanee was by all odds the most independent youngster of the family. His brothers and sisters, now full-grown, had long ago taken to themselves mates and settled down. Not so young Shanee.

But this season it was otherwise with Shanee. Casually observing the mating plan of all wild things, suggested to him his own loneliness. For the first time he took keen, new interest in certain handlike trails, the footprints of a possible companion.

Instinctively Shanee knew that somewhere she waited his coming, if only he could find her. Summer passed. Still he wandered alone. One memorable night, however, he hastily scratched his way down from his solitary nesting place in a big tamarack, where he had slept all day; for off to the south, borne upon the soft night air, came a whimpering, persuasive cry—the mating call of a young raccoon.

Like a streak of silver, Shanee tore his way through thickets of sharp briery cedars whose obstinate, prickly branches impeded him. He skipped lightly over bogs, across treacherous windfalls, fearing nothing. Occasionally he would halt to get his bearings and listen.

Once he thought that he had located her, this longed-for companion. But when he reached the spot, arriving with green-glowing eyes and swift heart, to his disgust he found that he had been misled by the quavering cry of a small owl.

Tonight, for a wonder, Shanee was not giving his entire mind to hunting food, his quest being of far greater importance. Muzzle to earth he ran, examining flat tracks of Owasse, the she-bear; seeing the deep holelike places where a lynx or bobcat had bounded across his path, or the cleft, sharp prints of deer hoofs. Then, suddenly, to his intense joy and excitement he found that which he sought—certain handlike tracks. These he recognized and immediately began to follow, whimpering under his breath as he ran.

Even before he reached the end of the trail, he heard the young raccoon call again, but this time her voice was not soft and beguiling. Its tone had changed to one of agony and fear.

Close beside a rock he found her, one foot caught in a rusty, abandoned trap. Two of her toes were held fast. Battering her young body about in agony, she struggled among rank ferns and pine needles, and at first she bared her teeth at Shanee. Soon, however, her fears changed to whimpers of pain and understanding, as with almost uncanny instinct Shanee frantically worked and tore at the trap, seeking to free her.

Finally the rusty bolts gave way, and suddenly she was free. Then together they stole away into the forest. Thus did Shanee Raccoon woo and win a mate.

* * * * *

They came out one night to a windswept hill. The moon was big—an ideal night for adventure. It chanced that around the bend of a brook, in a certain still, deep pool, Hushkoni was bathing her four kittens. The beautiful mother skunk stood upon a flat stone in the center of the pool, watching the black-and-white flashing forms, uttering occasional squeaks of admonishment. Curiosity being a predominant characteristic in Shanee's nature, no sooner had he glimpsed the four little skunks bathing than he forgot temporarily even his new mate.

Squatting down behind a conveniently low cedar bush, from where he could watch the skunk family without being seen, he stared at them, overcome by admiration for the pretty sight. Puppylike, he would twist his head from side to side in wonder at their antics, his green eyes sparkling. For in all Shanee's wanderings, never had he come so close to a skunk family. Soft as waving grain stirred by wind was the beautiful black-and-white pelt of Hushkoni. Her tail was a plume carried over her back.

Leaning over the pool, she pushed the little skunks back into the water as they tried to join her on a flat stone. Three of her litter finally succeeded in climbing out of the pool, but one, weaker than the others and heavy with water, fell back as he ventured to gain a foothold. Then, with infinite patience, the mother skunk reached over and tenderly lifted him forth by the nape of his neck, nosing him gently in the rear until he finally gained the bank, rejoining the family.

Like kittens at play, Hushkoni's brood began to frolic. Whereupon Shanee, forgetting all caution, crept stealthily forth from behind the cedar bush, watching with delight the baby skunks rolling over each other in joyous abandon among the jewelweed and mint.

Poor Shanee! He never understood what happened to him. Like magic, the skunk family disappeared, leaving inquisitive Shanee alone on the bank of the brook, uttering sharp cries of fear and torment as he tore madly at his smarting, skunk-gassed eyes and nose.

Rolling frantically among the bushes, vainly he tried to rid his beautiful fur coat of the sickening oily spray which covered him. All his washing, however, was vain. It would take weeks of purification and scouring to cleanse that fur. Thus Shanee, the dandy, the beau among the wild kindred, was sadly humiliated; he was no longer desirable.

Much to his chagrin, worse followed. His degradation was complete, for he lost favor with his newfound mate. When he reached home, with snarls of dislike and suspicion she flew at him, driving him forth. Thus once again Shanee became a bachelor wandering over the trails, forsaken and alone. He was miserably unhappy, for in all the woods there is nothing so disconsolate as a wandering, unmated raccoon.

* * * * *

The wild grapes were ripening, trailing serpentlike their festooned lengths as they meandered through dense swamp jungles. Mounting high, draping cedars and balsams, the vines hung heavy with thick-skinned, purple grapes. These days Shanee, the raccoon, shortened his naps. Even in his dreams he growled uneasily as, remembering the luscious hanging fruit, he feared perchance that some rival might strip the coveted vines before he reached them.

Squatting in the crotch of a tall cedar early one morning, Shanee feasted upon grapes. Frost had touched the fruit during the night, and Shanee's face appeared dipped in blood—the overripe fruit burst at a touch. The only thing which vexed him was armies of venomous, white-banded hornets and yellow jackets, tormenting him, boldly crawling over his sticky snout and into his eyes, making him growl crossly as he cuffed at them.

Shanee, being thoroughly engaged by all this, was unaware that his movements were being watched by a wild stranger far below. It was an enemy who stared up at him hatefully, uttering low growls. Owasse, the black bear, often came there to feed, as did others of the wild, but this creature who halted far below was squat of body, insolent, and clumsy. Although only about the size of a bulldog, he possessed more mean qualities and cruel ferocity than any other animal that followed the forest trails. It was old Carcajou himself, a wolverine.

Jealously, covetously, he watched Shanee at his feast far overhead. Finally unable to restrain his greed, the wolverine's cruel, ivory white nails commenced to pull his clumsy carcass up into the tree. Just then Shanee sighted him. Baring his teeth, the surprised raccoon humped his back boldly, as if to spring, standing his ground bravely as the wolverine came on.

Shanee was trapped. He had reached the end of the limb where he now clung. Suddenly, with a snarl of triumph, the wolverine leaped, and poor Shanee, missing his hold, crashed below with a thud. Meantime old Carcajou peered down at his rival, baring his teeth jubilantly as he fell to work among the vines.

Shanee was partially stunned by the fall, but soon rallied and streaked off into the woods, dragging one leg which was broken. Crawling into a sheltered windfall, he denned temporarily until his leg mended. Animals recuperate quickly in their wild state, and fortunately the raccoon's retreat was not far from water. Crawling to the pool, there lying half-submerged, Shanee dropped his plumy tail upon the surface of the water, allowing it to float. He was cunning enough when he saw one crayfish investigate his bait, to allow it to cling to his tail. One crayfish would attract others. Biding his time until he caught more, Shanee landed his entire catch, devouring them at leisure.

* * * * *

Again the decorative plan of nature changed. Between spired, black pines leaped forth torches of flaming maple. Poplars, golden-yellow, shimmered in the frosty air. On rounded foothills, velvety-green, a new growth of young spruce flaunted its colors. Cathedral-like balsams—blue-green, aromatic—ranged along the skyline. Blood-red sumacs and warm, brown bracken formed backgrounds.

Shanee hunted the swamps and forests, seeking his lost mate, who now had an interesting litter of four young raccoons. The grapes had gone, leaving behind bare, snaky vines. Still, Shanee fared well enough. He was putting on his hibernating fat; and when he scampered over the trails, his now-glossy coat shifted as he ran.

On a moonlight night Shanee took a new trail. The faint wash of tides lapped to and fro. Not far distant he saw the gleam of the sea, as the young moon left a path of silver across incoming tides. Shanee neared the inlets, where scrub pines came down to meet a sandy beach. Rhythmically the waves shifted shoals of little pebbles and small golden shells, which tinkled musically when released by the tide. Peevishly Kitami, the porcupine, broke the silences. Then Mankoke, the owl, already perched on her watchtower, sent a lonely call across the forest.

Single file, a mother raccoon led her young ones down a trail to the sea. They would feast there upon "coon oysters," small, salty bivalves which attach themselves to reefs and which may be reached at low tide. Capering across the sand, leaving behind their handlike, delicate footprints, the raccoon family advanced.

However, the small raccoons craved the more easily found sweet mussels, readily cracked by their sharp teeth and close at hand. But the mother raccoon swam out over the sand bar to the black, jagged reefs to seek the slippery rocks where grew larger shellfish.

Shanee, wandering afar off up the beach, suddenly glanced skyward. An ugly, black menacing cloud covered the moon. Offshore, whitecapped breakers dashed over the reefs with loud, angry roars. Soon the reefs would be under deep water. Then above the break, break of incoming tides Shanee heard distinctly the long, agonizing cry of a raccoon in distress.

He recognized that summons. It was the call of his lost mate. Again came the wailing, pitiful call for aid, but fainter. Shanee's mate was held prisoner out on the black reefs in the clutches of a giant oyster.

Shanee's wits did not desert him. A great wave aided him, and only just in time did he reach her. By a clever bit of surgery, delicately, swiftly, with his sharp teeth he severed the little black paw held in an oyster's mighty grip, and freed his mate. Not a second too soon, for as the two reunited wild things left the black reefs, an incoming wave dashed high above it.

Aided by tides, Shanee and his mate reached again the sandy beach where four whimpering, terrified raccoons sought their mother. And then, even before the beach was under water, the raccoon family was fast asleep in its home nest, while a storm rocked the tree.

* * * * *

"Shanee, Gallant Gentleman," by Jean M. Thompson. Published January 16, 1938, in Young People's Weekly. *Reprinted by permission of Joe Wheeler (P.O. Box 1246, Conifer, CO 80433) and Cook Communication Ministries, Colorado Springs, Colorado. Jean Thompson wrote for inspirational and popular magazines during the first half of the twentieth century.*

The Path of the Sky

Samuel Scoville Jr.

Four orphan ducklings decided Aunt Maria was their mother, and would never let her out of their sight. But then, one night, out of the sky descended a gorgeous emerald-headed drake from the far north—and nothing was ever the same after that. The setting: Connecticut during the time of World War I.

* * * * *

Deacon Jimmy Wadsworth was probably the most upright man in Cornwall. It was he who drove five miles one bitter winter night and woke up Silas Smith, who kept the store at Cornwall Bridge, to give him back three cents overchange. Silas's language, as he went back to bed, almost brought on a thaw. The deacon lived on the tip-top of the Cobble, one of the twenty-seven named hills of Cornwall, with Aunt Maria, his wife, Hen Root, his hired man, Nip Root, Hen's yellow dog—and the ducks. The deacon had rumpled white hair, a serene, clear-cut face, and, even when working, always wore a clean white shirt with a stiff bosom and no collar. Aunt Maria was one of the salt of the earth. She was spry and short, with a little face all wrinkled with goodwill and good works, and had twinkling eyes of horizon blue. If anyone was suddenly ill or had unexpected company or was getting married or buried, Aunt Maria was always on hand, helping. As for Hen, he cared more for his dog than he did for any human.

When a drive for the "Liberty Loan" was started in Cornwall, Hen bought a bond for himself and one for Nip and had the latter wear a Liberty Loan button in his collar.

Of course, the farm was cluttered up with horses, cows, chickens, and similar bric-a-brac, but the ducks were part of the household. It came about in this way: Rashe Howe, who hunted everything except work, had given the deacon a tame decoy duck who seemed to have passed her usefulness as a lure. It was evident, however, that she had been misleading Rashe, for before she had been on the farm a month, somewhere in sky or stream, she found a mate.

Later, down by the ice pond, she built a nest; a beautiful basin made of leaves and edged with soft down from her black-and-buff breast. There she laid ten blunt-ended brown eggs, which she brooded until she was carried off one night by a wandering fox. Her mate went back to the wilds, and Aunt Maria put the eggs under a big clucking Brahma hen, who hatched out four soft yellow ducklings. They had no more than come out of the shell when, with faint little quackings, they waddled out of the barnyard and started in single file for the pond. Although just hatched, each little duck knew its place in the line, and, from that day on, the order never changed. The old hen, clucking frantically, tried again and again to turn them back. Each time they scattered and, waddling past her, fell into line once more. When at last they reached the pond, their foster mother scurried back and forth, squawking warnings at the top of her voice; but one after another, each disobedient duckling plunged in with a bob of its turned-up tail, and the procession swam around and around the pond as if it would never stop.

This was too much for the old hen. She stood for a long minute watching the ungrateful brood, and then turned away and evidently disinherited them upon the spot. From that moment on, she gave up the duties of motherhood, stopped setting and clucking, and never again recognized her foster children, as they found out to their sorrow after their swim. All the rest of that day they plopped sadly after her, only to be received with pecks whenever they came too near. She would neither feed nor brood them, and when night came, they had to huddle in their deserted coop in a soft little heap, shivering and quacking beseechingly until daylight.

The next day Aunt Maria was moved by the sight of the four ducklings, weary, but still pursuing the indifferent hen, keeping up all the while a chorus of soft, sorrowful little quacking which ought to have touched their foster mother's heart—but didn't. By this time, they were so weak that if Aunt Maria had not taken them into the kitchen and fed them and covered them up in a basket of flannel, they would never have lived through the second night. Thereafter, the old kitchen became a nursery. Four human babies could hardly have called for more attention or made more trouble or have been better loved than those four fuzzy, soft, yellow ducklings.

In a few days the whole homelife on top of the Cobble centered around them. They needed so much nursing and petting and sooth-ing that it almost seemed to Aunt Maria as if a half-century had rolled back and that she was once more looking after babies long, long lost to her. Even old Hen became attached to them enough to cuff Nip violently when that pampered animal growled at the newcomers and showed signs of abolishing them. From that moment, Nip joined the Brahma hen in ignoring the ducklings completely. If any attention was shown them in his presence, he would stalk away majestically, as if overcome by astonishment that humans would devote their time to four yellow ducks instead of one yellow dog.

During the ducks' first days in the kitchen, someone had to be with them constantly. Otherwise, all four of them would go, *"Yip, yip, yip!"* at the top of their voices. As soon as anyone came to their cradle, or even spoke to them, they would snuggle down content-edly under the flannel and sing like a lot of little teakettles, making the same kind of a sleepy hum that a flock of wild mallards gives when they are sleeping far out on the water. They liked the deacon and Hen, but they *loved* Aunt Maria. In a few days, they followed her everywhere around the house and even out on the farm, paddling along just behind her in single file and quacking

vigorously if she walked too fast. One day she tried to slip out and go down to the sewing circle at Mrs. Miner Rogers' at the foot of the hill, but they were on her trail before she had taken ten steps. They followed her all the way there and stood with their bills pressed against the bay window, watching her as she sat in Mrs. Rogers' parlor. When they made up their minds that she had called long enough, they set up such a chorus of quacking and so embarrassed Aunt Maria that she had to come out.

"Those pesky ducks will quack their heads off if I don't leave," she explained shamefacedly.

The road uphill was a long, long trail for the ducklings. Every now and then they would stop and cry, with their pathetic little yipping note, and lie down flat on their backs and hold their soft little paddles straight up in the air to show how sore they were. The last half of the journey they made in Aunt Maria's apron, singing away contentedly as she plodded up the hill.

As they grew older they took an interest in everyone who came to the farm, and if they did not approve of the visitor, would quack deafeningly until he went away.

Once Aunt Maria happened to step suddenly around the corner of the house as a load of hay went past. Finding her gone, the ducks started solemnly down the road, following the hay wagon, evidently convinced that she was hidden somewhere beneath the load. They were almost out of sight when Aunt Maria called to them. At the first sound of her voice, they turned and hurried back, flapping their wings and waddling with all their might, quacking joyously as they came.

Aunt Maria and the flock had various little private games of their own. Whenever she sat down, they would tug at the neatly tied bows of her shoelaces until they had loosened them, whereupon she would jump up and rush at them, pretending great wrath, whereat they would scatter on all sides, quacking delightedly. When she turned back, they would form a circle around her, snuggling their soft necks against her gown, until she scratched each uplifted head softly. If she wore button shoes, they would pry away at the loose buttons and pretend to swallow them. When she was working in her flower garden, they would bother her by swallowing some of the smallest bulbs and snatching up and running away with larger ones. At other times they would hide in dark corners and rush out at her with loud and terrifying quacks, at which Aunt Maria would pretend to be much frightened and scuttle away pursued by the whole flock.

All three of the family were forever grumbling about the flock. To hear them, one would suppose that their whole lives were embittered by the trouble and expense of caring for a lot of useless, greedy ducks. Yet when Hen suggested roast duck for Thanksgiving, Deacon Jimmy and Aunt Maria lectured him so severely for his cruelty that he was glad to explain that he was only joking.

Once, when the ducks were sick, Hen dug angleworms for them all one winter afternoon in the corner of the pig pen where the ground still remained unfrozen, and Deacon Jimmy nearly bankrupted himself buying pickled oysters which he fed them as a tonic.

It was not long before they outgrew their baby clothes and wore the mottled brown of the mallard duck, with a dark, steel-blue bar edged with white on either wing. Blackie, the leader, evidently had a strain of black duck in her blood. She was larger and lacked the trim bearing of the aristocratic mallard. On the other hand, she had all the wariness and sagacity of the black duck, of whom there is no wiser bird.

As the winter came on, a coop was fixed up for them not far from the kitchen, where they slept on warm straw in the coldest weather with their heads tucked under their soft, down-lined wings up to their round, bright eyes. The first November snowstorm covered their coop out of sight; but when Aunt Maria called, they quacked a cheery answer back from under the drift.

Then came the drake, a gorgeous mallard with a head of emerald-green and snow-white collar and with black-white-gray-and-violet wings, in all the pride and beauty of his prime. A few days and nights before, he had been a part of the Far North—beyond the haunts of men, beyond the farthest forests where the sullen green of the pines gleamed against a silver sky, where a great wasteland stretched clear to the tundra, beyond which is the ice of the arctic. In this wilderness, where long leagues of rushes hissed and whispered to the wind, the drake had dwelt. Here and there were pools of green-gray water and beyond the rushes stretched the bleached brown reeds, deepening in the distance to a dark tan. In the summer, a heavy, sweet scent had hung over the marshland, like the breath of a herd of sleeping cattle. Here had lived uncounted multitudes of water fowl.

As the summer passed, a bitter wind howled like a wolf from the north, with the hiss of snow in its wings. Sometimes by day, when little flurries of snow whirled over the waving rushes, sometimes by night, when a misty moon struggled through a gray rack of cloud, long lines and crowded masses of waterbirds sprang into the air and started on the far journey southward. There were gaggles of wild geese flying in long wedges, with the strongest and the wisest gander leading the converging lines, wisps of snipe, and bands of duck of many kinds. The wigeons flew, with whistling wings, in long black streamers. The scaup came down the sky in dark masses, making a rippling purr as they flew. Here and there, scattered couples of blue-winged teal shot past the groups of slower ducks. Then down the sky, in a whizzing parallelogram, came a band of canvasbacks with long red heads and necks and gray-white backs. Moving at the rate of a hundred and sixty feet a second, they passed pintails, black ducks, and mergansers as if they had been anchored, grunting as they flew. When the rest of his folk sprang into the air, the mallard drake had refused to leave the cold pools and the whispering rushes. Late that season he had lost his mate; and lonely without her and hoping still for her return, he lingered—among the last to leave.

As the nights went by, the marshes became more and more deserted. Then there dawned a cold, turquoise day. The winding streams showed sheets of sapphire and pools of molten silver. That afternoon the sun, a vast globe of molten red, sank through an old-rose sky which slowly changed to a faint golden-green. For a moment it hung on the knife-edge of the world and then dipped down and was gone. Through the violet twilight, five gleaming, misty-white birds of an unearthly beauty—glorious trumpeter swans—flew across the western sky in strong, swift, majestic flight. As the shadows darkened like spilt ink, their clanging notes came down to the lonely drake. When the swans start south, it is no time for lesser folk to linger. The night was aflame with its million candles as he sprang into the air, circled once and again, and followed southward the moon path which lay like a long streamer of gold across the waste-lands. Night and day, and day and night, and night and day again, he flew, until, as he passed over the northwestern corner of Connecticut, that strange food sense, which a migrating bird has, brought him down from the upper sky into the one stretch of marshland that showed for miles around. It chanced to be close to the base of the Cobble.

All night long he fed full among the pools. Just as the first faint light showed in the eastern sky he climbed upon the top of an old muskrat house that showed above the reeds. At the first step there was a sharp click, the fierce grip of steel, and he was fast in one of Hen's traps. There the old man found him at sunrise and brought him home wrapped up in his coat, quacking, flapping, and fighting every foot of the way. An examination showed his leg to be unbroken, and Hen held him while Aunt Maria, with a pair of long shears, clipped his beautiful wings. Then, all gleaming green and violet, he was set down among the four ducks who had been watching him admiringly. The second he was loosed, he gave his strong wings a flap that should have lifted him high above the hateful earth where tame folk set traps for wild folk. Instead of swooping toward the clouds, the clipped wings beat the air impotently and did not even raise his orange-webbed feet from the ground. Again and again the drake tried in vain to fly, only to realize at last that he was clipped and shamed and earthbound. Then for the first time he seemed to notice the four who stood by, watching him in silence. To them he fiercely quacked and quacked and quacked, and Aunt Maria had an uneasy feeling that she and her shears were the subject of his remarks. Suddenly he stopped, and all five started toward their winter quarters; and lo and behold, at the head of the procession marched the gleaming drake with the deposed Blackie trailing meekly in second place. From that day forth he was their leader, nor did he forget his wrongs.

The sight of Aunt Maria was always the signal for a burst of impassioned quacking. Soon it became evident that the ducks were reluctantly convinced that the gentle little woman had been guilty of a great crime, and more and more they began to shun her. There were no more games and walks and caressing. Instead, the four followed the drake's lead in avoiding as far as possible humans who trapped and clipped the people of the air.

At first, the deacon put the whole flock in a great pen where the young calves were kept in spring, fearing lest the drake might wander away. This, of course, was no imprisonment to the four ducks, who could fly over the highest fence. The first morning after they had been penned, they all sprang over the fence and started for the pond, quacking to the drake to follow. When he quacked back that he could not, the flock returned and showed him again and again how easy it was to fly over the fence. At last, he evidently made them understand that for him, flying was impossible. Several times they started for the pond, but each time at a quack from the drake they came back. It was Blackie who finally solved the difficulty. Flying back over the fence, she found a place where a box stood near one of the sides of the pen. Climbing up on top of this, she fluttered to the top rail. The drake clambered up on the box and tried to follow. As he was scrambling up the fence, with desperate flapping of his disabled wings, Blackie and the others, who had joined her on the top rail, reached down and pulled him upward with tremendous tugs from their flat bills until he finally scrambled to the top and was safely over. For several days this went on, and the flock would help him out and back into the pen every day as they went to and from the pond. When at last Aunt Maria saw this experiment in prison-breaking, she threw open the gate wide, and thereafter the drake had the freedom of the farm with the others. As the days went by, he seemed to become more reconciled to his fate and at times would even take food from Aunt Maria's hands, yet a certain reserve and withdrawal on the part of the whole flock was always apparent to vex her.

At last, just when it seemed as if winter would never go, spring came. There were flocks of wild geese beating, beating, beating up the sky, never soaring, never resting, thrusting their way north in a great black-and-white wedge, out-flying spring, and often finding lakes and marshes still locked against them.

Then from the sky came the strange wild call of the killdeer, who wore two black rings around his white breast, and the air was full of robin notes and bluebird calls and the shrill high notes of the hylas. On the sides of the Cobble the bloodroot bloomed, with its snowy petals and heart of gold and root dripping with burning, bitter blood—frail flowers which the wind kisses and kills. Then the beech trees turned all lavender-brown and silver, and the fields of April wheat made patches of brilliant velvet-green. At last there came a day blurred with glory, when the grass was a green blaze and the woods dripped green and the new leaves of the apple trees were like tiny jets of green flame among the pink-and-white blossoms. The sky was full of waterfowl going north.

All that day the drake had been uneasy. One by one, he had molted his clipped wing feathers, and the long curved quills, which had been his glory, had come back again. Late in the afternoon, as he was leading his flock toward the kitchen, a great hubbub of calls and cries floated down from the afternoon sky. The whole upper air was black with ducks. There were teal, wood ducks, baldpates, black duck, pintails, little blue-bills, whistlers, and suddenly a great mass of mallards, the green heads of the drakes gleaming against the sky. As they flew, they quacked down to the little earthbound group below. Suddenly the great drake seemed to realize that his power was upon him once more. With a great sweep of his lustrous wings, he launched himself forth into the air in a long, arrowy curve and shot up through the sky toward the disappearing company—and not alone. Even as he left the ground, before Aunt Maria's astonished eyes, faithful, clumsy, wary Blackie sprang into the air after him, and with the strong awkward flight of the black duck, which plows its way through the air by main strength, she overtook her leader, and the two were lost in the distant sky.

Aunt Maria took what comfort she could from the three that remained, but only now that they had gone did she realize how dear to her had been Greentop, the beautiful, wild, resentful drake, and Blackie, awkward, wise, resourceful Blackie. The flock, too, was lost without them, and took chances and overlooked dangers which they never would have been allowed to do under the reign of their lost king and queen. At last fate overtook them one dark night when they were sleeping out. That vampire of the darkness, a wandering mink, came upon them. With their passing went something of love and hope, which left the Cobble a very lonely place for the three old people.

As the nights grew longer, Aunt Maria would often dream that she heard the happy little flock singing like teakettles in their basket or that she heard them quack from their coop—and would call out to comfort them. Yet always it was only a dream.

Then the cold came, and one night a great storm of snow and sleet broke over the Cobble, and the wind howled as it did the night before the drake was found. Suddenly Aunt Maria started out of her warm bed and listened. When she was sure she was not dreaming, she awakened the deacon, and through the darkness they hurried down to the door, from the other side of which sounded tumultuous and familiar quacking. With trembling hands she lighted the lamp, and as they threw open the door, in marched a procession. It was headed by Greentop, resentful and reserved no more, but quacking joyously at the sight of light and shelter. Back of him, Blackie's soft, dark head rubbed lovingly against Aunt Maria's trembling knees with the little caressing, crooning note which Blackie always made when she wanted to be petted. Back of her, quacking embarrassedly, waddled four more ducks, who showed their youth by their size and the newness of their feathering. Greentop and Blackie had come back, bringing their family with them. The tumult and the shouting aroused old Hen, who hurried down in his night clothes. These, by the way, were the same as his day clothes except for the shoes, for, as Hen said, he could not be bothered with dressing and undressing except during the bathing season, which was long past.

"Well, if it ain't them pesky ducks again!" he said, grinning happily.

"That's what it be," responded Deacon Jimmy. "I don't suppose now we'll have a moment's peace."

"Yes, it's them good-for-nothin'. . . " began Aunt Maria, but she gulped, and something warm and wet trickled down her wrinkled cheeks as she stooped and pulled two dear-loved heads, one green and the other black, into her arms.

* * * * *

"The Path of the Sky," by Samuel Scoville Jr. Published March 1918 in St. Nicholas. *Samuel Scoville (1872–1950), born in Norwich, New York, primarily wrote books for young people and books about nature.*

THE SNAKE THAT CAME TO THE RESCUE

Oliver D. Schock

Is it possible to find any good qualities in an untamable animal such as a snake?
Read on. . . .

* * * * *

Snakes. Ow-w-w! Horrid things. Poisonous, slimy, crawling, treacherous creatures. Now, do not tell me there is anything nice to be said about them!

But that is where you are wrong.

It is queer how many people dislike snakes. They loathe and fear them above anything else and rush for a heavy stone or stick to kill one which crosses their path. They do not know there are quite as many good snakes as bad ones, and that, in Pennsylvania at least, there are only two kinds, copperheads and rattlesnakes, which are venomous; while there are a dozen others which render great help to the farmer by eating rats, mice, harmful insects, grubs, and worms, and are perfectly harmless to man. The snake-hunters must inherit, deep down in their natures, the horror which came to Mother Eve, in the Garden of Eden, when after she had eaten the apple, and knew at once the wrong she had done, she looked into the wicked little eyes of the serpent who had tempted her to disobedience.

The big blacksnake, sometimes six feet long, does seem a very unpleasant and threatening individual to meet when walking in the woods and gives boys looking for birds' nests many a scare, which serves them right, if they are stealing eggs. But though he does eat young robins and catbirds, he also destroys much vermin, and is not really an enemy of mankind, unless attacked or cornered, when he will defend himself, just like any other animal. Even then, his bite is not serious. Snakes, you know, generally travel in pairs, and when you find Mr. Snake, you can be pretty sure that Mrs. Snake is somewhere near.

This story is about two blacksnakes which were seen by a State Highway Official, while he was inspecting a recently completed job in Somerset County.

As he drove along the pleasant mountain road, he was surprised to see in the path ahead of him, two large snakes coiled together. He

wondered if they had been fighting, and stopped his car and went cautiously ahead on foot to find out. As he came near, he found that the smaller one had been run over by a passing automobile, and was unable to move. The other snake had wrapped itself around the uninjured part of its crippled companion, and was plainly making an effort to drag her into the long grass at the side of the road, where she would be out of further danger. As the inspector poked gently at the two, in his wish to understand the queer situation, Mr. Snake took alarm and slid off into the bushes. So the man, thinking the other was dead anyway, went on about his business. Returning an hour later, what do you think he saw? Mr. Snake had come back, and was again twined around the limp form of his mate, seeking once more to carry her away to safety.

The inspector stood for several moments, quietly watching them, and thinking. *I take off my hat to you, Mr. Snake,* he said to himself. *You are just a snake, but you have shown love for your mate, have tried to help her when she was hurt, and have persisted in your plan, even though a stupid man interfered. Your friend is dead, but I will render you the only service in my power.*

He took a stick and lifted the bruised reptile carefully onto the wayside grass, and then, still thoughtfully, went on down the mountain.

* * * * *

"The Snake That Came to the Rescue," by Oliver D. Schock. Included in Curtis Wager-Smith's Animal Pals (Philadelphia: Macrae Smith Company, 1924). If anyone can provide knowledge of the earliest publication of this story, please send the information to Joe Wheeler (P.O. Box 1246, Conifer, CO 80433).

The Peacemaker

Frank Lillie Pollock

Have you ever wondered about whether or not bull moose ever get their antlers stuck together during fall mating season? Every so often it happens, but few humans ever see it because predators such as wolves or mountain lions usually close in and kill the helpless bulls.

But one man—a forest ranger—awoke one night to the sounds of a violent duel between two bull moose not far away.

Very quietly and fearfully, he decided to investigate.

* * * * *

Scott Caldwell was a forest ranger at Algonquin National Park which lies between the Ottawa River and Lake Huron, and his duties were to look out for fires, kill wolves whenever he got a chance, keep the canoe routes open, and warn off unlawful hunters, for no shooting is permitted in that immense game preserve.

It was the end of September, and the mosquitoes and sand flies had ceased to make the woods unendurable. Scott had been following a chain of small lakes in his canoe, and at night he camped at the same spot where he had camped on his round of a month before.

Before he turned into his blankets, he heard the bellow of a bull moose somewhere, far away across the forest—a vast grumbling thunder, more charged with primeval savagery than any other sound of the wilderness. He had heard that sound almost every night for two weeks. The park was full of moose that had grown very bold after a couple of generations' safety from rifles. It was their mating season, and the bulls were challenging each other, and fighting savagely.

Scott went to sleep, but was awakened before dawn by a tremendous uproar. He jumped out of his blankets and put his head out of the tent. It was a brilliant, windless night, with moonlight almost as bright as day, and away across the yellow autumn ridges there was a noise of furious smashing and tearing among the brush, mingled with savage grunting and roars, and a sharp, recurrent clash and rattle. It was somewhere down the lake; it did not sound more than a quarter of a mile away.

As soon as he got the sleep out of his eyes, Scott realized what it was. A couple of bull moose must be fighting it out. Few men have ever witnessed such a duel, and Scott was keenly anxious to see it. He looked at his watch; it was after three in the morning, and after listening a little longer to the thrilling sounds, he took his rifle, launched his canoe, and paddled down along the shore.

He thought he might be able to see the fight from the water, but when he drew opposite the noise, it was apparent that the animals were a hundred yards or so inland. He got to shore, therefore, and stole in through the cedar thickets, holding his rifle ready for self-defense in case one of the maddened animals should charge him.

Suddenly, the sounds of battle ceased. Scott halted, listened, and waited. He thought he heard an occasional stamping, but the fight seemed over. He advanced a few yards farther, cautiously, and then stopped with a paralyzing shock of fright.

Not twenty feet from him were two moose, looming black and gigantic over the scrubby thickets; they were standing motionless, with lowered heads close together, face to face.

For a moment Scott was afraid even to breathe. The moose did not move, and he ventured to take a step backward. A stick crashed under his boot-heel, and at the sound, both moose plunged and leaped from side to side, but without separating their heads. The broad prongs of horn creaked and rattled together.

Scott stood still, astonished at their queer behavior, but presently he perceived the reason of it. The prongs of the bulls had become interlocked, so that the fighters were unable to disengage themselves.

It is a mishap that occurs not infrequently to fighting moose and deer. The timber wolves usually finish off such helpless victims very quickly, and woodsmen now and again pick up a pair of great skulls with the antlers still fast locked together.

With more assurance Scott examined the trapped warriors at close range. One was an old bull, standing full seven feet to the top of his humped shoulders, with a superb spread of polished ebony-dark horn. The other, a smaller and probably younger animal, had a great jagged gash across his flank that still dripped dark blotches on the pine needles.

They both wrestled and roared as the ranger approached, wrenching their antlers desperately, but they could not break loose. Scott was struck with pity. He could not leave the splendid animals to the first wolf pack that passed. It was part of his duty to protect game in the park, and he decided to wait till morning to see if he could not find some means of disentangling them.

So he sat down at the foot of a tree and waited for daylight. The moose moved restlessly about, butting and tugging alternately and striking at each other with their forefeet. Probably each accused the other of holding him. Presently the larger bull stumbled and fell, dragging his antagonist with him, and they kicked vainly in the endeavor to get up again, till at last they lay quiet on their sides, apparently tired out.

With the earliest light Scott examined them more closely. The prongs of the smaller bull had been forced between those of his antagonist by a tremendous effort, and the broad antlers were so entangled that nothing short of a saw or a lever could get them free.

Scott had no saw, and would have hesitated to go so near the animals if he had, but with a long lever he thought that he could do the work. The moose could not get up nor move much, and so long as he kept out of reach of their sharp forefeet, he would be in no danger.

He paddled hurriedly back to camp and got his ax. When he returned, the moose lay as he had left them. He cut a sapling about ten feet long and as thick as his arm, and trimmed it, sharpening one end. With this formidable lever he approached the panting bulls and rather nervously tried to insert the point between the locked prongs.

But at the first touch of the pole the animals fell into such a wild and sudden panic that he retreated hastily. They roared, kicked, and squirmed and writhed about the ground with the pine needles flying in clouds. It was too violent a convulsion to last long, and in a minute or two they lay quiet again, heaving, exhausted, and quelled for the moment—Scott thought.

He came up again, on the side opposite the dangerous hooves, and once more tried to force the sharpened pole between the tangled antlers. Again and again, he failed as the moose jerked their heads aside, but finally, with a quick thrust he managed to insert the lever in the right place, and threw his weight on the other end.

The tough horn creaked and bent, but so did the lever. The large moose jerked his head violently—there was a snap, and his head was free. Almost before Scott could realize that he had succeeded, the smaller bull had sprung up and vanished into the woods like a brown flash, with a scattering of dead leaves.

Then the big bull jumped up as if he had been raised by a spring, and before Scott could leap aside, he was knocked headlong into a clump of hemlock ten feet away by a single sweep of the broad antlers. Luckily, it was only a glancing blow or it would have crushed his ribs. Scott scarcely understood what had happened before the bull crashed into the hemlock like a locomotive with a bellow that fairly chilled Scott's backbone.

The moose was stopped by the elastic resistance of the shrubs, and Scott, who had been pitched into the middle of three or four small trees, scuttled into the densest corner like a scared rabbit.

The bull roared savagely, with outstretched neck. Scott was far from expecting any such ingratitude for all his pains, and when he realized the situation he was very angry. If he had had his rifle he would have shot the beast at once, but he had laid down the weapon somewhere out of sight.

The moose sniffed noisily into the thicket, and tried to strike the ranger with its front hooves. The blows came crashing through the branches, but Scott was able to dodge them by wriggling to the other side of the clump. This game could not last long, however, and while he watched his enemy he cast rapid glances about for some safer refuge.

Twenty yards away, a great cedar had fallen with its top lodged among the branches of a beech. Its trunk sloped from the ground to a height of twenty or thirty feet, and Scott perceived that if he could reach the butt, he could run up the sloping trunk, and be out of danger in a moment.

The difficulty was to reach it. But a swift thrust of a hoof that missed his shoulder by an inch warned him that he would have to attempt it. He crawled nearer the edge of his covert, on the side farthest from the moose, gathered his legs tensely under him, and at a favorable moment he sprang out and ran.

A crash told him that the bull was at his heels. He dodged round one side of a large pine as the moose plowed past on the other. As the animal charged blindly back again, Scott again slipped aside and made another bolt for his tree.

He reached it this time, by the margin of a second, for the bull's antlers clattered against the trunk and almost knocked him off as he ran up its slope. After the first couple of yards, the cedar was closely set with rusty branches, and they tore his clothes as he forced his way up the swaying trunk.

For the trunk swayed and gave as he climbed it. The bull following him underneath, butted it hard and shook it from end to end. Evidently its top was only very slightly caught in the beech that supported it.

Scott had not climbed halfway to the top of the tangled trunk, when he felt a dangerous yielding under his feet. There was a great sustained, increasing crackle and crash from the top, and it sank under him.

Scott gave one terrified glance down at the bull waiting almost below. He made a spasmodic effort to jump aside, but the branches held him, and the cedar went sailing down and completed its long-interrupted descent in a tremendous shock, smashing against the earth.

The shock drove him deep among the branches, tearing his face and hands, and he tried to wriggle deeper yet. He expected the bull to plunge upon him the next instant. Blinded among the twigs, he could see nothing, but in a few seconds he was aware of a great smashing and struggling that was shaking the whole mass of the fallen tree.

He disengaged himself from the branches. The moose was not visible, but down in the heavy cedar-top, Scott saw a furiously struggling mass of dark hair and the black tip of a shovel-shaped horn.

The bull had been caught by the falling tree and buried among the branches. When he peered into the tangle, Scott thought that the animal was pinned down by the trunk, but had been saved from crushing by the mass of limbs. The bull was safe enough now, however, and perfectly incapable of getting out.

Scott felt no great pity for it, and went back to camp with his rifle and ropes. The next day, however, he returned to the place with an ax, intending to chop the animal free.

He found four timber wolves sitting on their haunches around the tree, waiting patiently till the bull should cease to struggle, or till they overcame their dread of a trap. They bolted at Scott's appearance, too quickly for him to get a shot, and he chopped the moose out of the branches.

The animal was subdued at last. When it was free, it struggled painfully to its feet, gazed anxiously at Scott, and made its way limpingly down to a little stream and drank for a long time. Then, while Scott watched, it seemed to melt into the woods with the speed and silence of a shadow.

* * * * *

"The Peacmaker," by Frank Lillie Pollock. Published September 1908 in St. Nicholas. *Frank Pollock wrote around the turn of the twentieth century.*

HILARY'S SIX LITTLE PIGS

George Ethelbert Walsh

The six little razorback piglets were cute when small, but big-time trouble when they got older. Finally, they'd destroyed so much property that Hilary gave up on ever getting his investment back. The Florida swamp was the place for the likes of them.

Time passed. One day when Hilary was in the swamp cutting logs, he heard a sound that froze his blood.

* * * * *

Hilary's pigs were "poor, common trash," as they say in the South, and were little better than the semi-wild razorbacks, which roam at will through the pine woods and low swamps of Florida. But they had been carefully reared by the boy, who, among other tricks, had taught them to respond to his calls.

"Piggy! Piggy!" was not an attractive call from one point of view, but it

always acted like magic upon the six little razorbacks. The reason for this was that Hilary always rewarded them with some toothsome food when they responded promptly.

Hilary expected to make enough from the litter to start himself on the road to a fortune by the next year, when he intended to purchase fruit trees and begin his orange grove. His father had promised him the land, and had given him the pigs to raise. The growth and development of the animals consequently formed a matter of daily importance to the boy. He watched them, played with them, and admired them until they were more like pets than practical farm animals to fill somebody's pork barrel later.

There were three white pigs, two mottled brown and white, and one black. The latter was always the scamp of the litter, and if any mischief was brewing, Hilary watched the black pig and waited for developments. He knew that if it was held under control, the others could be trusted.

But the blood of their wild ancestors showed itself more or less in all of the pigs as they grew older, and they made Hilary work for the money he intended to reap from their dead carcasses. Such simple things as breaking into the cornfield and destroying the stalks, or running away and hiding for days in the swamp, were scarcely worth chronicling. These accidents Hilary expected, and he took them as a matter of course.

But when one day six pigs walked up to the house and grunted dismally, and Hilary looked out and saw that every one was painted a bright green, his heart misgave him. For a moment he was so overcome by the sight that he laughed outright, exclaiming aloud, "Look at the green pigs! Where did they find all that paint?"

"That isn't paint," said his father, in a moment. "They've been at that Paris green I left in the potato field." Then looking seriously at Hilary, he added, "I'm afraid that's the last of your pigs, Hilary. They must have taken enough inside to poison them."

Hilary said nothing, but believed as his father did. Nevertheless, he held them under the pump and deluged them with water until some of the green was washed off. The pigs liked this less than the dose of Paris green and squealed continually during the process.

Instead of dying, the whole litter seemed to thrive on the Paris green, and by the time the last vestiges of the poison had worn off they were fatter and heavier than ever. For a few days they were quiet and kept out of mischief. Then, led by their little black companion, they resorted to other mischievous tricks and escapades, which brought down anger upon their heads.

Late one evening queer noises sounded on the cellar stairs, followed by a rumbling sound as if barrels were being rolled down the steps. At first, thoughts of ghosts and burglars alarmed Hilary and his parents, and they started for the cellar with a lantern and gun. But before the door was open somebody said, "I'll bet it's Hilary's pigs up to more mischief."

This proved true, for when they investigated they found six porkers in the cellar busily engaged in devouring a load of cabbages that had been stored there the day before. How the animals had broken loose from their pen, shoved open the cellar door, and tumbled down the steps, are all problems that are not easy to solve. They were in the cellar, however, and it took two hours to catch them and carry them, one by one, to the surface of the earth again, all squealing until the nearest neighbor came running to the rescue.

"Thought you were having a midnight pig-sticking," he said, when matters were explained. "If I were you, I'd sell those pigs right away."

"Who'd buy them?" asked Hilary.

"Nobody, I guess, unless he wanted 'em for a circus."

They were too small to kill, and they had eaten so much that something had to be done with them to recover the money already expended in raising them.

"It isn't only what they have eaten," said Hilary ruefully, a few weeks after this, "but it's what they have damaged. I guess if I paid you for all the injury they have done, I'd be out of pocket now."

"It was well that I didn't put that in the bargain," replied his father with an amused smile. "How much damage do you suppose they have caused?"

"I can tell you," responded the boy, taking a paper from his pocket. "Here it is. I've kept account of it all."

He pushed the paper before his father, on which was plainly written:

June 10—Damage to corn field and fence: $1.50

June 10—Damage to barn by rooting under the foundation: $2.00

June 15—Destruction of ten gallons of Paris green: $2.50

June 20—For destroying a hundred cabbages: $2.00

For sundries, torn trousers, broken fences, shoe leather, etc.: $5.00

Total: $13.00

"I think that will cover most of the damages," added Hilary, "and at that rate they are a losing venture. I am already in debt to you."

"Then you propose to turn them over to me?"

"Yes, if you will take them."

"But if I don't want them, what then?"

"We shall have to sell them or kill them."

There was silence, and then Hilary's father said, "We won't kill them now or give them away; that would be poor business policy. Besides, it wouldn't be just to the pigs. We must let them have every opportunity to redeem themselves. We must give them another chance."

"What do you propose to do?" asked Hilary, interested in the new plan, but not sure of what his father meant.

"We'll turn them over to nature. Their ancestors were wild razorbacks, and it is evident the wild blood is in them and that we can't civilize them. We'll brand them with some mark and turn them loose in the swamp, where they can forage for themselves. If they live, we will round them up next winter and kill them for market."

"They will hardly seem like my pigs," remarked Hilary, a little ruefully, remembering the many good times he had had with the pigs when they were young. "If they were not so bad, I'd try them again on the farm."

He was half inclined to give the animals another trial, but early next morning he was startled by a noise near the barn. Hurrying out, he was greeted by a chorus of wild squeals. His pigs were in trouble again.

All except the black leader were covered with half-slaked lime, which had poured over them from an overturned tub, where his father had put it in the morning to prepare for whitewashing the cellar. The little black leader had escaped harm, but the others were covered with the burning stuff. For hours they squealed and grunted around, until every hair was burnt off their bodies.

"That settles it," said Hilary to himself.

On the following day, the pigs were branded with the letter H, and then they were conducted to the swamp and banished forever. They were so fond of this swamp that there was little danger of their ever returning voluntarily to the farm.

Although banished from the farm and deprived of the corn and other delicate food that had been fed to them in the past, the pigs seemed perfectly content, wallowing in the muck and dirt and eating the wild plants, acorns, and roots. Hilary went down to the swamp nearly every day to watch them, occasionally carrying corn for them to eat. Not once did they attempt to return to the forbidden land—not even to play some prank upon their owner.

A month after their banishment, Hilary was in the swamp cutting logs to make box-staves with, when he met with a queer experience. He had crossed a wet, marshy place near a lagoon, when suddenly he heard an ominous hissing all around him. That warning was well known to him, and he stood perfectly still.

The Florida diamondback rattlesnake is a dangerous creature to anger, and when he announces his presence by a rattle, it is safe to stand perfectly still until the creature can be located. In a few moments

Hilary caught sight of the rattler a dozen feet in front of him, with head erect and body coiled ready for a spring.

The boy would have backed cautiously away, but behind him he had heard another rattle. He knew that the mate of the big fellow was somewhere near him in the rear, and he was almost paralyzed with fear.

For nearly five minutes he stood, facing the snake, and straining his ears to catch the rattle behind him. It was a fearful position, and any sudden movement on his part probably meant death. He could almost hear his heart beat, so great was his excitement.

Then suddenly, to relieve the strain, there was a crash in the bushes in front, and a black head protruded, followed by several white ones. Then came a series of grunts. Hilary recognized his six pigs, now grown fat and strong; and they apparently knew him.

For a moment the boy's attention was diverted from the snakes to the pigs, then he opened his mouth and called.

The six porkers had not forgotten the rewards that always followed this call, and with almost a simultaneous bound they dashed through the bushes toward the boy. They came onward like a whirlwind, startling the snakes so that they turned around to face this unknown danger. As the pigs dashed past them, the rattlers struck out at the charging enemy, but instantly realizing their mistake, tried to slink away.

With a grunt of satisfaction, the black porker caught sight of the rattlers, and then dashed at them, followed by the whole litter. It was in vain that the snakes squirmed and struck at their new enemies. With sharp hoofs, the pigs trampled them to pieces and so mutilated their bodies that they were hardly recognizable.

When they were through, Hilary was ready to fall upon his banished pigs and pet them; but they were averse to petting and stood their distance. Nevertheless, he promised them the biggest dinner of choice corn and cabbages the next day that he could collect.

That night he said to his father, "I guess we can wipe out the damages in that bill. The pigs were worth more than thirteen dollars to me today."

"Yes, and a hundred times thirteen," replied his father, with a faint indication of moisture in his eyes.

And so Hilary's pigs were considered a good investment, in spite of mischievous tricks and pranks.

Note: Florida's razorback hogs are immune to the rattlesnake's poison and are their deadliest enemies in the swamps.

* * * * *

"Hilary's Six Little Pigs," by George Ethelbert Walsh. Published October 21, 1901, in Nor-West Farmer. *George E. Walsh (1865–1941), was born in Brooklyn, New York, and wrote during the late nineteenth and early twentieth centuries.*

TONG KAAM

Adeline K. MacGilvary

* * * * *

Bennie was eight and small for his age, and the Prince's wicked peacock, Tong Kaam, was big. Not just big, but a continual source of terror and torment.
If only Bennie could strike back!

Bennie Bristow sometimes wished he wasn't a minister's son, especially a missionary minister's son. You see, one has to be extra good if one is a minister's son—that is, if your dad happens to be a missionary, too, you're expected to be tactful on top of that! Bennie would have liked to stop being a missionary's son for about an hour—or until he could settle old Tong Kaam.

Trouble was Tong Kaam belonged to Chow Luang, the "Big Prince" of the reigning royal family, and it would never do for a missionary's son to be tactless to the peacock of Chow Luang! He was old and wicked, was that peacock, and in his own way and sphere, the greatest tyrant that ever lived. He used to fly over into the Bristow yard and destroy fruit and vegetables and flowers and scare the little flock of ducks almost into fits. It was his way of showing his authority, or immunity, because, of course, he knew that nobody dared to hurt him.

As for poor Bennie, Tong Kaam was a perfect terror to that boy! Bennie was only eight and small for his age, and the peacock was big and old and strong, and a heathen, too, I'm sure; for if he ever happened to see the little boy playing in the yard, he would steal up from behind and do his best to make a hole in Bennie's head. Bennie had to keep his weather eye open, believe me, and if he saw the peacock coming, he'd race for the house and slam the door shut after him.

"Most every day, when he's flying over to the little island in the river after the cucumbers they've just planted over there, he stops at our house and chases me," Bennie told his mother, adding confidently, "I'd certainly like to hit him with a rock!"

"No, no, Bennie," his mother said hastily. "He's the prince's peacock, and nobody ever dares molest him. Now, if I were you and saw the peacock coming, I'd just go away!"

"Oh, I do go away!" replied Bennie. "I'd better, too, or he'd soon kick me to death, I guess!"

"I'm afraid you've been teasing him," said Bennie's mother, who didn't know quite how wicked the old bird was.

Not long after this, little Bennie was sitting in front of the house on Kaam Tip's head. Kaam Tip was Bennie's father's elephant, a respectable, decent beast. Bennie would tap her on the knee and up would go her leg, and on it Bennie would climb, catching hold of the elephant's collar and swinging himself up on her head. There sat Bennie, his bare legs tucked behind the big, soft ears, pretending he was a king riding at the head of his army, when—*Whir! Rustle! Flap!* Full tilt came old Tong Kaam, his wings all ruffled, his tail spread, crying, *"Mow-meow!"*

Taking flight and sailing upward, he aimed straight at the little boy, who didn't have the ghost of a chance to get away, perched up there on Kaam Tip's head.

"Go 'way, you old rascal!" shouted Bennie, ducking his head and throwing up his arm to protect himself from the peacock's cruel spurs. "Catch him, Kaam Tip! Catch him by the tail!"

Kaam Tip's big trunk flew up just in time to get a nasty whack, right on the sensitive part, from Tong Kaam's spur. With a snort of surprise, the elephant rolled her little eyes at the wicked peacock. Bennie began to shout for help, and had slipped his right leg over, ready to jump to the ground, when the elephant began to run.

There was a tiny rope, like a clothesline, fastened to Kaam Tip's hind leg, but it was only put there as a matter of form, to make Kaam Tip think she was tied. The huge animal snapped it like a bit of thread; in fact, she forgot she was tied and did not even feel the rope snap. Off she raced through a grove of banana trees, brushing over like a blade of grass any tree that happened to be in the way.

At first little Bennie could only cling on tight and get his right leg carefully behind Kaam Tip's ear. Then he began to think. *Kaam Tip is running away. She mustn't do that!*

"Stop, thou foolish elephant!" he cried, in the elephant's native language. "Stop now, stop!"

Kaam Tip was a very good elephant. She soon slowed down; and when she felt Bennie's hand slap her right temple, she turned to the left, as she knew she should, and soon she was headed home again. They had gone quite a distance, though, and when they reached the Bristow house, there stood Bennie's father on the veranda, looking around for his elephant.

"Kaam Tip ran away," said Bennie, as he rode up. "That old peacock scared her."

"Well, I'm glad you brought her back," remarked Mr. Bristow, who was in a hurry. "I have to ride her to town now."

Bennie got off and stood on the veranda watching his father and the elephant driver roll grandly away on Kaam Tip, and wishing he could go too.

It was awfully hot, and Bennie thought he would go down to the river nearby and paddle. He had hardly reached the bank, shaded by banyan trees, when he spied his old enemy sunning himself on the little cucumber island in the river.

I'd better go away, thought Bennie. *That is, if he sees me.*

Tong Kaam had seen Bennie; but, being very wicked, he pretended he hadn't. So Bennie began paddling, and when the peacock thought the boy wasn't watching anymore, he made a sudden swoop from the island. Bennie scrambled out of the water and began to race for home. *Whir! Whir! Flap!* came Tong Kaam, *mow-meowing* furiously. Bennie was a good sprinter and reached the house safely, but he tripped on the veranda steps. *Whack!* Down came the peacock's spurs on the boy's head!

Bennie scrambled into the house and slammed the door. There was a patch of red on his short, light hair, and he put his hand up and felt something wet, and when he looked, his fingers were red too. With a dismal howl, he ran to find his mother. (Sometimes even a big boy may be excused for howling.) When his mother heard the story and saw the nasty wound on poor Bennie's head, her patience quite gave way.

"It's a shame, I do declare!" she exclaimed. "Next time that bird chases you, just pick up a stick or anything and give it to him! I won't have a horrid peacock bullying my little son!"

Quite comforted, and bandaged up like a war hero, Bennie sat on the veranda and thought long thoughts of revenge, while he ate a juicy mango. But there was one thing Bennie hadn't told his mother—he was afraid of the peacock! That night he had his familiar nightmare: Tong Kaam miles high and ruffled up, chased him up and down narrow winding stairs all night! So the next time he saw the peacock coming, he ran away as fast as he could.

It was another hot, hot day, like most days in Siam, and Bennie went to the well for a drink. Even the singing lizards' voices sounded tired and stuffy, and everybody was lying under a mosquito net trying to sleep and forget how uncomfortable it was. Bennie had just taken the coconut dipper by its long teak handle and was about to dip up a nice, cool drink, when—*Whir!* Tong Kaam suddenly swooped down from a caster oil tree close by.

Bennie looked wildly around. The peacock was between him and the house, and he couldn't rightly jump down the well. In fact, he was trapped.

"Mow! Mow!" screamed Tong Kaam as he dashed at Bennie.

Then something happened. Bennie himself didn't know how, exactly. He says he swung the coconut dipper around and around by the handle, and suddenly it hit Tong Kaam in the neck. The next minute the peacock lay on the grass, quite still, with his eyes closed.

Bennie looked and thought, *I guess he's dead, but I don't care!* Calmly, he took a drink and then walked away to the river bank, there to paddle in peace.

But Tong Kaam wasn't dead. He had only fainted. He soon came to and stood a long time fixing his crumpled feathers before staggering off home.

* * * * *

The next day when Bennie saw his old enemy, there was no whir, no rush. Tong Kaam, in fact, sidled respectfully away, and when Bennie shouted, "Hey, get out of those beans!" he sheepishly obeyed.

The natives, who suffered from the awful bird's visits to their cucumber gardens, soon heard of Bennie's power over him, and sometimes they would come and ask the little boy to make the royal peacock go away. Bennie always did it gladly, waving his arms and shouting like a general, "Scat you old rascal, and be quick about it too, or I'll go and get the coconut dipper!" At which Tong Kaam would flutter home with a hangdog expression on his haughty face.

* * * * *

"Tong Kaam," by Adeline K. MacGilvary. Published May 1918 in St. Nicholas. *Adeline MacGilvary wrote during the first quarter of the twentieth century.*

A Coyote Named Promise

Penny Porter

"Look, it's over, and she's dead," he said. "All we can do now is watch for the buzzards to circle around and pinpoint where her body is." And so it began.

* * * * *

I awoke to a violent, unearthly cry—like the sobs of a tortured demon.

At Singing Valley Ranch, night sounds are common: the screech of a great horned owl, the yowl of a bobcat, the electrifying squeal of bats racing the dawn. But for sheer shock value, nothing could equal this terrifying din of voices right beneath my window. It made me sit bolt upright in bed, my heart pounding. The clamor was soul-piercing—and unmistakable. Coyotes!

The coyote's eleven-note voice ranges from a high-pitched, hysterical shriek to a low, haunting howl. A single animal can sound like a pack of eight, two like sixteen, and when the voices of four echo against the distant mountains and cliffs it's like a symphony gone wild.

At Singing Valley Ranch, we rarely saw a coyote. It might have been because a Mexican lobo had staked out our land a long time ago and kept the coyotes at bay. Or maybe we ourselves had simply frightened coyotes off with our noisy all-terrain motorcycles.

Whatever the reason, I found myself missing the magic of this shy, illusive creature gliding through the tall gamma grasses or slinking among our manzanita bushes. Although hunger prompted his predatory ways, the coyote had become a dim memory for my husband, Bill, and me—except on moonlit nights when an eerie howl resonated from far off arroyos and mountain tops, reminding us he was still out there somewhere.

Now, as the fiendish howls reached an ear-splitting crescendo, I sat a long moment in bed. Then, as quickly as all the commotion started, it stopped. I reached over and pulled back the edge of the striped serape covering the window, expecting to see a battleground strewn with dead cats, dogs, chickens—perhaps a newborn calf. Instead, a telltale quivering of pyracantha bushes, a scattering of orange-red berries and tufts of rabbit fur strewn like dandelion down provided the only vague clues to one of nature's desperate struggles for survival.

There had been a coyote out there—I knew this for sure. My gaze shifted to Bill on his tractor over a mile away. His headlights were still on as the early morning mist crawled over the lush green fields. He'd been cutting alfalfa since four in the morning, and the day before he'd oiled, tightened, and sharpened the sixty-three sets of gleaming, scissorlike blades on the swather, a sixteen-foot-long mower he attached to the side of the tractor with the help of our grown son, Scott. I wondered, *Did he see the animal?* The tractor vanished into the ghostly fog.

The coyote was far from my thoughts as I prepared breakfast for Becky and Jaymee, now twelve and nine. They had been outside feeding their 4-H calves and rabbits before school. Suddenly, Jaymee burst into the kitchen, horror in her eyes. "Mama!" she yelled. "Daddy killed a coyote! Just now, out in the field; I saw it thrown in the air!"

My thoughts flew back to those frenzied howls of less than two hours before. They still sent a chill through me. Could that have been the animal Bill had killed? "Are you sure?" I asked Jaymee, trying to ease her fears. "You know for sure it was a coyote? You were so little when they used to be around here."

"But I know what coyotes look like!" Jaymee persisted. "I saw one on the highway, and when Becky and I were riding with Scott near the mountains, we saw two of them. They were gray and brown and black with huge, bushy tails and just a little smaller than a German shepherd." A deep frown angled between her eyebrows. "I know what one looks like, Mama. And this was a coyote."

Much later, when Bill came in for breakfast he hung his sweat-stained hat on the rack and sank into his chair by the wood stove. "I think I clobbered a coyote," he said.

"I know. Jaymee told me." I could see how much this bothered him.

"For the past few days, I've seen a coyote watching me from the edge of the field—a pitiful-looking creature, scrawny and sick. I saw her once in the rearview mirror catching mice behind the baler. She didn't seem the least bit afraid. Now this had to happen." He was silent for a moment. "I looked all over for her, but she must have dragged herself off and died in some other part of the field."

"How do you know it was a 'she'?"

"Big old belly," he said, sighing. "Pregnant."

I shuddered. "Maybe you just thought you killed her."

He shot me a hard glance. "Look, it's over, and she's dead," he said. "All we can do now is watch for the buzzards to circle around and pinpoint where her body is. Then I'll get rid of it before cutting and baling the rest of the field."

The buzzards, however, never appeared. *Could the coyote still be alive?* I wondered. *Maybe it's still out there somewhere, suffering.* I couldn't stop thinking about it.

Summer slipped into autumn, and thoughts of the coyote dimmed. Winter closed in. Now hunger stalked the wild animals on the surrounding desert. In search of food, they moved closer to our barns, corrals, and outbuildings. Often at night, while checking on pregnant heifers for signs of labor, I caught sight of a hooded skunk, or a coatimundi (a monkey-like animal of the raccoon family), or a

porcupine emerging for a starlit shuffle searching for a forgotten kernel of corn or a tree where a few remaining leaves or a cocoon could be found.

January arrived with a vengeance, bringing icy winds, heat lamps in the henhouse, a need for blankets on the horses, the calving season—and the return of the coyote. It was midnight when I heard the first diabolical shrieks and howls near my chicken coop. I dressed quickly and dashed outside. There in the beam of my light, I met her face to face—an old coyote with three legs. The left hind leg was missing below the knee.

So Bill's tractor took only her leg, I thought. *But how did she survive? Could she still catch a rabbit?* She was less than a shadow, a pathetic, skeletal creature with coarse, gray ratty-looking fur. The once-bushy tail was mangy and shredded, and she looked at me with such a woebegone expression it tore at my heart.

And what about her baby? If it had lived, the pup would be weaned by now and was probably eight or nine months old. I glanced around but didn't see it.

Enormous ears cupped the coyote's dainty, intelligent face. Although she showed neither fear nor surprise, I sensed something was terribly wrong. Then she tilted her head into the shaft of light, and I saw her aged amber eyes. Veiled in cataracts, they glowed like tiny blue gas jets in the darkness. *Poor, poor thing,* I thought. *That's why she got hurt. She's probably blind.*

I wanted to reach out, step a little closer, but this was a wild thing. *Can she see at all?* I wondered.

As if in answer to my thoughts, her lips parted, revealing a flash of smile—and fangs. I knew now she could see something, but I also sensed she was not alone because she was reacting like any mother animal would, protecting her young against strangers. Perhaps her pup was nearby.

We stared at each other, neither of us moving, until gradually I felt a rare bond of trust pass between us before she finally turned and hobbled off into the night. At that moment, I grasped the full extent of the tragedy that had befallen her. Maybe Bill was right. Perhaps we should have hunted her down and put her out of her misery. Overwhelmed with pity, I flicked off the light so she could shrink unobserved into the moonlit shadows.

What can I do? I asked myself. I didn't care that she was a predator and a threat to small livestock. She was starving to death. Her natural diet was birds, rodents, rabbits, and insects. But I had also heard that coyotes like fruit. *Maybe she'll eat dog food with apple slices on top,* I thought.

I couldn't help wondering what Duke would think of that. Duke was our timid, 206-pound English mastiff, and he ate and slept on the front porch only a few feet from where this same coyote had killed a rabbit all those months before. He let the barn cats finish his food, but how would he feel about this wild animal eating from his bowl? I had to try. So I prepared the first bowlful.

A short time later, back in bed, I heard strange sounds outside the front door. Peeking beneath the striped serape, I saw the wild and the tame, hair raised, tails clamped, cowering on opposite sides of the bowl. Although a single lunge from Duke could crush the crippled coyote, the confrontation unleashed a torrent of voices instead. The coyote, ears pinned back and crouched low on her belly, was yapping and scolding while Duke, afraid to take his eyes off her, trembled and whined. Finally, he sank heavily to the ground, dropped his huge head between his paws, and moaned while the coyote crept toward his bowl and dug in.

When I told Bill the good news, he shook his head. "It's not right," he said. "This is a wild animal that's now weak and can't take care of herself. We should put her out of her misery—or at least let nature take its course. We shouldn't be interfering."

"She has survived this long," I countered. "If it's survival of the fittest, maybe she is the fittest! We're just giving her a little help."

Several times during the following three months, the coyote appeared. And as she fed at Duke's bowl, I was always aware of a mournful howl from the barren plains to the north. Could it be her pup crying for her? Or possibly the father of her pup? Coyotes mate for life, and the yearning wail was almost heart-moving in its plea.

Eight weeks after her first feeding at Duke's bowl, I noticed a glint of brownish red and black tinting her silver-gray fur. And her body was filling out a little more. One morning I told the girls, "Our coyote looks much healthier. I think she's going to make it!"

"You promise?" Becky asked.

"Promise," I said, crossing my fingers. But the same question still nagged. As Bill had said, was it really fair to interfere with the laws of nature and prolong a life of agony? I was still searching for an answer when Jaymee, who liked to give every living creature on the ranch a name, smiled at me. "Oh, Mama," she said. "That's perfect. Let's call her 'Promise.'"

An unusually wet spring brought swarms of flying beetles, moths, and flies that clung to the screen door like barnacles. When they started slipping into the house every time the door opened, Bill installed a zapper light. When the bugs hit the electrically charged mesh, they sparked and fizzed, then spiraled down onto the concrete in smoldering piles. Barn cats arrived in droves to feast on them.

Then one evening, before I'd put extra food out for Promise, the familiar shrieking and yodeling began. We all peered through the living-room window and saw Promise snapping eagerly at the smoking bugs in midair and gobbling them down.

"I'll bet she likes them cooked, better than raw," Jaymee murmured, and I saw Bill peer over the top of his newspaper. The laughter in his eyes said he was becoming more and more intrigued by this animal he didn't think should survive, but had survived. A few days later, he bought a book that told us how, in times of drought and famine, the cunning coyote will outlast all creatures because he is a digger of wells. When smaller animals and birds come to his well to drink, the coyote pounces.

Promise appeared only one more night after that, and I saw she was pregnant again. Her fur was thick and shiny now, her tail magnificently bushy.

From Bill's book, we learned that Promise—being pregnant—was the number-one female of her pack, the only one producing offspring. Experts believe the lead female emits a hormonal odor that induces other females not to ovulate.

Late in her pregnancy, the coyote holes up in a den burrowed by a smaller animal and now revamped it to suit her size and needs. There she is fed by her mate and other members of the pack—but only until her pups are weaned. After that, Promise would be on her own again.

Soon I noticed a change in Bill. It began one day when he left a patch of alfalfa uncut. "Another dumb duck built her nest out there," he mumbled. Then a week later a jackrabbit sat in the alfalfa and defied him. So once more, Bill's straight-arrow cutting veered off at an angle.

Finally, one scorching day in August, Bill had an even bigger surprise while he was baling. A three-legged coyote appeared on the edge of the field—with a young pup. Promise hobbled toward the tractor, totally unafraid.

As Bill watched, a memorable thing happened. When the baler scooped up the windrows, field mice suddenly lost their hiding places beneath the rows of neatly stacked hay, and the coyote pup began chasing them. After the pup had eaten several mice, Promise waited until he caught another—then she grabbed her offspring by the neck and threw him to the ground. He let go of the mouse in his mouth, and she ate it herself. As mother and son took off single file and lay down near the edge of the field, Bill marveled at what he'd seen.

"Did they go to sleep?" Becky asked at dinner that evening when Bill told us the story.

"Not right away," he said, "at least, not the pup." Now his voice took on a new, warmer tone when he talked about the mother and baby coyote. "He had to chew on her nose for a while, nipped at her ears and face. But he finally curled up right next to her and settled down. She looked so content, just like your Mama did when you kids were little and finally fell asleep." Bill glanced at me and grinned.

As winter approached, we wondered what would happen when our crippled coyote weaned her pup and the pack no longer took special care of her. Would she turn to us again?

Each night, I put extra food in Duke's bowl with slices of apple on top. It was still there in the morning. But distant howling and shrieking were more prevalent than in the past. Was it Promise? Her two pups? Her pack?

The months hurried by, and alfalfa season came again. More and more, Bill's quarter-mile windrows zigged and zagged. When I commented on the scattered patches of uncut green dotted with lavender blossoms, he grumbled, "I had to steer around a quail's nest and a couple of dumb rabbits." But the sudden twinkle in his eyes said a few detours were OK.

It was near the end of April when he saw a coyote bounding along beside him, inches from the razor-sharp blades. It was a female—young, healthy, and pregnant. "She followed me for over an hour," Bill told us. "She wasn't the least bit scared of me or the tractor. And she caught mice like an old pro."